WILLOW PATTERN WALKABOUT

Text © 1959 Edward B. Kirwan Ward
Illustrations © Paul Rigby

ISBN-13: 978-988-18667-1-4

© 2011 Earnshaw Books

Willow Pattern Walkabout was first published in 1959 by West Australian Newspaper (Perth).

HISTORY / Asia / China

EB042

Published by Earnshaw Books Ltd. (Hong Kong)

WILLOW PATTERN PATTERN WALKABOUT

Kirwan Ward and Paul Rigby

photo courtesy of Jeremy Kirwan Ward

Foreword
By Graham Earnshaw

China in the 1950s was about as isolated a place as any in the world. You would have had to be someone truly strange, like an Australian, to get inside.

It was the height of the Cold War and, following the Communist Party's victory in 1949, the West's hundred-year grip on China's economy had been forcibly removed. In 1950, war broke out in the Korean Peninsula, and Communist China became an international pariah.

In the late 1950s, Chiang Kai-Shek and the Nationalists, who had been supported by America in China's civil war, were still counting on the West to support them in an invasion of the Chinese mainland.

After three years of the killing in Korea, the rest of the world had generally followed the US lead and rejected the New China. The New China, meanwhile, and in particular Chairman Mao, took the position that they no longer needed the rest of the world. The Chinese Communist Party, it was declared, would destroy the past and build the People's China in its place. The people of China, to a large extent, responded by saying, "Okay, let's give it a try." After a hundred years of chaos, a change surely couldn't be all that bad.

So China disappeared behind the "Bamboo Curtain". The nation became almost entirely inaccessible with the world having almost no sense of what was going on within its borders. All that reached the outside world were propaganda blasts about happy peasants and smiling workers in the form of red-cheeked, muscular individuals. China wanted itself to be seen as a socialist-communist paradise, where people lived simple yet clean and honest lives. No one could counter this image with an alternative view, because no one with any credibility could get in.

Near the end of the 1950s, the Communist Party launched its ambitious – and ultimately disastrous – Great Leap Forward, attempting to industrialize the country almost overnight. For a short moment, China reconsidered its isolationist stance and considered proving itself to the world. It decided to selectively reopen the doors and see who showed up.

Along came Kirwan Ward and Paul Rigby from *The West Australian* newspaper.

Australia, while basically in the Western camp – they had fought as part of the UN forces in the Korean War – always had about it a feeling of independence about it. It was sort of like the West's Yugoslavia. There was a sense that it was likely to be more impartial in its observations of China than the war-mongering Americans or the imperialist British. So perhaps it was on this basis, or perhaps some other basis, that the decision was made to approve the visas of two journalists from Australia.

In just about any respect, Ward and Rigby were as unlikely a duo to be granted visas to communist China in 1957 as could be imagined. They were best known back home for their satirical work and tart opinion pieces. That they were invited to visit Red China at that time and to be given the kind of access that they were granted for a period of several weeks was extraordinary.

What came out of their visit is a valuable record of an era that is, for almost all of us, just a blank. The book *Willow Pattern Walkabout*, first published in

photo courtesy of Jeremy Kirwan Ward

1958 and almost immediately forgotten, works because it was created with detachment and an objectivity that just about anyone from other parts of the English-speaking world in that era would have been incapable of. Ward and Rigby get to the heart of what China was at the time, and also what China is eternally. The team may have been best known for their humor, and they do poke fun at China from time to time, but it's a very gentle poke. They are never vicious in their depiction of the China and their jokes are more playful than cruel. There is an underlying dispassionate sense of respect.

Kirwan Ward, responsible for the words, does a remarkable job of stepping outside of his Western comfort zone and providing a narrative that is as perceptive as it is humorous, skeptical without being overly judgmental. In one passage he riffs on the absurdity of a state effort to eradicate sparrows from Beijing. Just pages later he cannot help but share his sincere admiration for a nation that is literally moving mountains to provide their children with a brighter future.

The accompanying cartoons by Paul Rigby are just superb; the work of a sensitive, talented artist looking at and recording China with a Western perspective. The average cartoonist at a major international newspaper of the day would have treated a Chinese communist subject in terms of evil dragons taking over the world, or perhaps a nasty racial caricature. There is nothing nasty in Rigby's drawings. His work exudes the same gentleness that pervades the entire work. Regardless of the era, these are wonderful drawings depicting China in a way that stands the test of time. I knew Paul through my father Arnold Earnshaw and the originals of some of these drawings adorned the walls of my father's home for many years. That is one of the reasons why I am proud to be able to resurrect this work.

The book reflects the eternal soul of China, but some of the scenes in *Willow Pattern Walkabout* are also very much related to that specific moment in time, China's period of isolation that lasted for nearly 30 years. There is a wonderful cartoon of a hotel in Canton at night. I saw that same scene in 1979, when I first came here. The streets of China's cities at that time were ink black. You approached your hotel in a rattly Shanghai sedan car, traveling down deserted streets and deposited at an entrance lit with one gloomy light bulb. There was a sense of complete otherworldliness about it, almost a 19th century feel. Rigby and Ward capture it perfectly.

One thing that Ward and Rigby did not have, of course, was a sense of the trajectory of the political movements and upheavals they witnessed. The chaos was just beginning, and there is no sense in this book of the incredible damage that was to be done to China throughout the Great Leap Forward and the Cultural Revolution of the late 1960s. The seeds and signs of this they missed, because they were carefully chaperoned around the sensitive bits by their state minders. No one they met would have talked to them about the negative aspects of what was going on, either, because China was already a highly controlled police state. Today, we are used to Chinese people talking to journalists about just about anything, but that was not the case when Ward and Rigby were here in the 1950s, or when I arrived here in 1979.

So even though they missed the seeds of the desperately negative events that were to darken and damn China in the decades ahead, the brilliance with which they portray what they *did* see is undeniable. As a small example, Rigby's depiction of "Ms. Peking 1958" is a simply wonderful juxtaposition of China as it was then compared to the rest of the world. You look at that picture and it's impossible not to smile.

It is an honor to republish this forgotten and fascinating work, *Willow Pattern Walkabout,* because of the great writing and drawings, because of the uniqueness of its perspective, and because it throws light on a dark and largely untouched era of China's history. I commend it to all readers.

Graham Earnshaw
Shanghai, December 2010

Kirwan Ward (left) and Paul Rigby returning to Australia from their tour of China, June 1958

"Which way to the Salt mines, mate?"

If you are so far over on the Right or Left wings that, from where you sit, you can't see the middle, you're not going to like this book. Before the mad mullahs of McCarthyism have flipped half a dozen pages they are going to find some sentence, some cartoon that doesn't unequivocally ridicule, or damn, China, and they're going to holler "The poor suckers have fallen for the old conducted-tour confidence trick; they've been brainwashed."

And the foam-flecked members of the lunatically Left soapbox set, noticing the odd hint, here and there, that Mao the messiah hasn't yet led his people to a party paradise, are going to set up the squawk that we are nothing but the hired lackeys of capitalism.

We have compiled our report of what we saw in China in the belief that there are important numbers of sane people in the centre who still like to hear both sides of any story.

Kirwan Ward   *Paul Rigby*

DAILY NEWS
Perth, Western Australia, March, 1959.

FOR THE little green train from Kowloon this was the end of the line. From Lo Wu, where the train stops, to Shumchun is only a couple of hundred yards, and a child could pitch a stone across the innocent brown creek that separates them, but, this little stream is a barrier as significant as the widest ocean, or the tallest, cloud-draped mountain range. With utter finality it rules a rigid line between one world and another. For Lo Wu is in the New Territories of Britain's Hong Kong, and Shumchun is in Red China.

Dead ahead the black girders of an ugly railway bridge made a solemn job of spanning the muddy mountain brook, beyond which a huge red flag, speckled with the five gold stars of the People's Republic of China, billowed above the tower of a concrete blockhouse and sunlight suddenly pinpointed the glint of binoculars trained on us as we moved forward to knock timidly on China's front door.

There is always a dry-mouthed tension when you cross a foreign border, and in this taut atmosphere it is fatally easy to over-dramatise the

situation; but this was undeniably a big moment. It was the moment we had waited for during the seven edgy months it had taken Peking's Foreign Affairs department to answer our letters and impatient cables. Our country, like America, still refuses China official recognition, so there were no amiable consuls in our hometown, or even in our own land, whom we could approach for visas. We had to apply direct to Peking and Peking, whether it is dealing with reporters or rajahs, just won't be rushed.

Crunching along the gravel beside the railway line, following the track worn by the restless feet of the world's transients, we could see khaki uniforms and steel helmets ahead. A tough little Mongolian soldier in a shapeless tunic, and over-large, sagging pants moved across to block our path, the blunt snout of a Russian sub-machine gun poking menacingly over his shoulder.

He looked grim and suspicious, but, surprisingly, he grinned, murmured "Good morning," flipped casually through our passports, then stood aside like a gracious host inviting guests to come in. We were in China, just like that. And the step that moved us past that sentry was as startling as the one Lewis Carroll's Alice made that drowsy summer afternoon when she stepped through the looking-glass.

It took us into an astonishing land where crime is almost extinct; where scrupulous honesty in small matters is palpably prevalent and where street urchins indignantly call a cop if you toss them a coin. A land that knows nothing about the mammary mountains of Mansfield, the ghost of James Dean, Lone Ranger or the horrors of hit

parades. A land without singing commercials, blackboard jungles, Private Presley, Miltowns, and juvenile delinquents. A land where the old brass deities have been sternly pushed away into the shadows of museums, and replaced by shoddy gilded plaster casts of the new Buddha in a boiler suit . . . Mao Tse-tung. A land where 600,000,000 people swarming over a land mass as big as all Europe, and hopelessly divided by centuries of materialism and misrule, have in nine fantastic years been somehow blended into the world's most dedicated, starry-eyed nation.

But there was no way of knowing all this as we stood in the sticky sunshine on the long, bare platform at Shumchun.

All we knew was that we had just handed over our precious passports and all our money to an impassive stranger who had given us no indication as to when we would get them back, if ever. Temporarily we were stateless and bankrupt. We looked back longingly across the bridge and wondered how, a long seven months, or a bare five minutes ago, this journey could have seemed to be such a wonderful idea.

Presently he was back with passports, and a fistful of the curious little scraps of paper and aluminium coins which are the new China's currency. (Less than a quarter of the population can read, so the smaller bills aren't marked in figures, as fives, tens, twenties; instead they have symbols that the peasants can understand, tractors, trains, and ships.) He was courteous and efficient, he called us "sir," not "comrade," and the baggage men who hustled up to handle our gear were like all other baggage men the world over, except for one staggering difference; these incredible guys refused a tip as if it were a test-tube full of bacteria. We figured that there must surely be something awfully screwy about a country where baggage men treat a tip

"Okay, I give in – I DID drop a cigarette butt."

that way, and we caught the Canton express determined to discover just what that something was.

According to the standard script a Red agent should have slunk up behind us the moment we set foot in the dreaded Mao-mau territory. Right away some eager-Geiger should have been searching for our tiny brains, scheming to send them to the laundry and a secret service man should have tailed us like a shadow. It would have given the thing a nice touch of adventure, but, almost disappointingly, it didn't happen that way. A young desperately busy, English-speaking Intourist man bought our tickets for us, checked our baggage aboard, shooed a couple of poker-faced peasants out of our seats, shook hands, and abruptly disappeared from our lives forever.

To travellers from our particular section of the western world, where timetable is a bad word and where schedules tend to be as elastic as Gertie's garter, there is one tricky and confusing feature about China's trains. They depart and arrive dead on time.

At 1450 hours precisely there came a sudden shattering bellow of Russian martial music and we rolled smoothly off towards Canton.

It has to be Russian music of course, because the peaceful bamboo beat was never meant for marching. The terrifying, brassy, bullying roar of the radio shouted down the minor rumblings of the train, swamping us with sound, browbeating us, making conversation impossible.

In sixty seconds flat the nerve war was over and lost. Our minds were jelly, cravenly eager to do anything that would ensure us two minutes silence. We glanced despairingly at the other passengers; after all this was their country, surely they weren't going to take this brutal standover stuff lying down? Surely some furious citizen, outraged at this monstrous mental intrusion, would spring up and rip the plug from the wall? We looked in vain; their faces were as serene as bronze Buddhas, as if they were deep in quiet contemplation upon some tranquil mountain top. Or as if nature had placed a protective layer, calloused and tough as a firewalker's foot, over their minds.

When the record scratched to a stop it was like losing

altitude quickly in a non-pressurised plane. Our ears clicked and hurt with decibel decompression, as the ordinary, welcome sounds rushed in. But then the radio was on again. Now a shrill little shrew of a woman announcer took over, and began haranguing us in the hectoring tones of a female top-sergeant bawling out a batch of trembling recruits in the bull ring. Her words, amplified to maximum volume, screeched through the shuddering compartment like high velocity shells.

We found a Hong Kong friend who makes regular business sorties to Canton, tapped him on the knee, and yelled:

"What's she talking about?"

Leaning over to within two inches of our aching ears he shouted: "Slogans; pep talk about keeping the train clean, swatting flies, and mosquitoes, killing mice, and chasing sparrows. All part of the Rectification campaign . . ."

He filled his lungs for another big competitive effort against the diabolical din: "You'll get used to it," he said, fortissimo. He was wrong, we never did.

In Red China the end almost always justifies the means; right now the leaders are obsessed with the determination to keep their new China clean, and they are succeeding spectacularly. In mud-walled villages where bantam fowls stroll in and out of front doors you see farmers' wives earnestly brushing the earthen floors with home-made switch brooms; and on the swirling brown rivers you see women who live their whole sad lives aboard reeking sampans, solemnly dipping rags in the muddy water and hopefully scrubbing the splintered soap boxes that are the family furniture.

Every few minutes, as we travelled strictly on schedule to Canton, uniformed attendants bustled anxiously through the compartment, probing beneath our feet with brooms; running damp cloths over unresponsive, yellowing woodwork; flicking reproving dusters over worn, leather upholstery that will never shine again. If your mind needs a little vigorous exercise to hold off fatty degeneration a short while longer, why not give it a workout on the thought of a country where the national pastime, pride, and habit, for young and old of both sexes, is spitting, but where a dead match on a train floor is a scandal? Balance that one and you have balanced your first entry in the bewildering Chinese ledger.

Remember the story of the walrus and the carpenter who became gravely concerned about the superabundance of sand on the seashore? The walrus put forward the tentative suggestion that seven maids with seven mops, sweeping for half a year might sweep it clear; but the carpenter (who was something of a realist) doubted whether the scheme was feasible, and he shed a bitter tear. You wouldn't catch the Chinese shedding any

bitter tears over a proposition like that. It wouldn't faze them for a second. What they would do would be to conscript seven million maids with seven million mops, and with a mixture of sweet-talk and intimidation, inspire them to go to work with such passionate energy that by nightfall, as sure as there's a banished Buddha in the Temple of Heaven, that seashore would be innocent of the tiniest speck of sand, and there would be nothing left but clean, shiny rock. When confronted with an impossible task China just gathers up another million workers, and the job shrinks overnight from impossibility to probability, to certainty, to achievement. All our lives we've been told that faith can move mountains and all our adult lives we have had it mentally filed with the Santa Claus thesis for veracity, but now, with our travel-traumatic eyes, we have seen the awesome ferocity of faith at work . . . we have seen the mountains move.

"Welcome to the Love-The-Masses Hotel—Canton's gayest."

CANTON:

We never did get to know his name and he remained anxiously anonymous, humbly happy to be just one six millionth part of dedicated zeal in the overwhelming human powerhouse that is modern China. We called him Sam.

He met us as we climbed down from the train at Canton; a slim, scholarly sort of chap of about 28, wearing a grey cotton tunic (the city was soggy with humidity), grey cotton pants, and soft black wing-wah slippers. He spoke the precise, pedantic English that a man learns in foreign classrooms but nowhere else.

Sam swiftly mustered our baggage, and gave us the first of the thousand surprises that we were due to meet in this strange awesome land. In a place like this, bristling with aggressive equality, we had thought that no man would stoop to such a menial task as carrying a visitor's bags so we seized ours manfully, but Sam vetoed the move in horror. In all my journeyings I have made it a fixed rule never to surrender my typewriter to anyone: strangers tend to regard it as some sort of indestructible projectile, they treat it as Parry O'Brien treats a sixteen-pound shot, and I protect it from porters like a bear guarding her cub. But Sam had it away from me in a flash. He whipped our passports in and out from under the nose of a white-jacketed security cop, bundled us into a Polish-made taxi, and headed us for our Canton home, the Love-The-Masses hotel.

We have, in our time, lived briefly in a great many hotels. Coming in from rain-soaked outback tracks, we have known the chilling welcome of bush boarding houses when the

cook's gone on a three-day jag and the yardman has forgotten to stoke the boilers. We have weathered the gloom of early morning air-arrivals in many a grey town, but never have either of us known anything like the clammy depression that smothered us as the Love-The-Masses loomed up. Probably we have lived too long in cities, still untouched by age, where the buildings are clean and white; where glittering glass facades dazzle the eye, for on this humid evening, this towering, grey hotel was unquestionably the most melancholy pile of masonry in our experience. The lobby looked like the entrance hall to the world's dreariest railroad station, washed with a wan yellow smear that was an economic compromise between light and darkness. There may have been a time when this place was gay as a Christmas tree, alive with colour, vibrant with the chatter of voices. Now it was old and shabby, grim as a county gaol.

Sam shook hands politely, tried a smile as tentative as that of a frontier sentry forbidden to fraternise, then merged with the steamy gloom of the Cantonese night. We were free to go where we liked; no restrictions, no briefings, and no one apparently taking the smallest notice of us. It was a hollow anti-climax to the bamboo-curtain complex built up by the long months of waiting for a visa.

Canton by day is a place of parks and gardens, with the great opaque Pearl River sliding swiftly by its doorstep. By night it is as austere as a blacked-out wartime city cowering under the constant threat of bombardment. Only an occasional street light challenges the night. Now and then a bus rumbles along, unlit inside, and carrying headlights as dim as a camper's hurricane lamp; but there is almost no traffic other than the flitting shadows of bicycles. We went cautiously along the broad waterfront street, as conspicuous in our western style clothes as if picked out by powerful spotlights, but nobody showed any curiosity, and though we met no other Europeans all night, no head turned, no eye flickered. Either through caution or courtesy, this is strictly a mind-your-own-business town.

Ahead, at last, there were lights. This was what Sam had told us about, the big deal, the People's Cultural Park. You pay your few cents by holding out a handful of flimsy, toy-like currency to the grave, capable little girl with twin plaits who seems to preside over every turnstile in China, and suddenly you're up to your ears in package-deal culture. These people are being taught to think about culture the way they used to think about rice.

"You check the Russian film with the Chinese sub-titles while I investigate the goldfish."

You gobble up as much of the stuff as is put before you and look for more. It is a strange and thought-provoking sight to see hordes of sampan dwellers, who are going home to sup on seaweed on two square feet of damp deck, catching up on a few centuries back log of culture by staring at goldfish; watching Russian movies (with Cantonese sub-titles hoisted jerkily on a sort of sail affair beside the screen), or following on a huge board the moves of a chess game. Under a dim rotunda an earnest comrade lectured an audience as animated as cigar-store Indians; and in the halls inside flashing-eyed teenager guides conducted stolid groups through an exhibition of spies, and enemies of the people. There were camouflaged parachutes, suitcases with false bottoms, sub-machine guns, pistols, concealed radio sets, all the standard spy equipment. And to tidy up each exhibit there was always a photograph of the spy or reactionary, or smuggler, staring bug-eyed at the camera and holding, at a convenient angle for easy reading, his signed confession. On the

walls were poster-style murals showing fearless Chinese soldiery capturing enemies . . . and the features of the hated foe were Western features.

All along the dark avenues of the park, silent groups moved from one exhibit to the next. At home, in any similar place, the people would have been rowdy and the park would have been littered with orange peel, cartons, and cigarette butts. Here the relentless culture-seekers trod as sedately as pall-bearers. Never a voice was raised; and the lawns were as free from rubbish as Wimbledon's centre court.

Only one person looked directly at us for more than a flick of the eyes. He murmured "Tovarich," but we shook our heads indignantly and he faded back into the margin of deeper darkness at the edge of the avenue.

A Soviet amazon girl strode out on to a large well-lit, open-air stage like an inflexible Joan of Arc leading her troops to battle, and the boards shivered beneath the thump of her jackboots. She wore a trim khaki military tunic with shining Sam Browne, and a blue serge skirt pleated like a Scotsman's kilt. Her job was to announce the next number. She barked it out unsmilingly, curt as a barrack square order, wheeled smartly, and stamped off leaving the quivering microphone to a similarly clad comrade with an excellent voice who sung without any gestures some earnest incomprehensible song. Her last strong note bugle-called out across the black park, she clicked her heels, about-turned and marched off. It was much more like a changing of the guard than a concert. No one clapped or murmured.

I peered through the dimness at the rows of serious

faces turned towards the stage. There was no visible expression of any kind. No pleasure, no displeasure, no joy, no sadness. Either these people just hadn't got the message or else they play culture deadpan in these parts.

If the old China was a duller, unhappier spot to live in (and the evidence in that direction is piling up convincingly) then it must have been a sad, sad land indeed and some sort of social upheaval was long overdue.

Next morning Sam was eagerly on hand to guide-dog us along the tourist trail through the memorial gardens erected to the memory of the 72 martyrs (China's civil war was fought between the martyrs and the reactionaries. The martyrs won, so they rate a tomb, but dead reactionaries have to settle for a hole in the ground, and most reactionaries are very dead indeed by now). He showed us museums and galleries till the mustiness seeped into our minds.

From under the ornate eaves and curling gables of an emperor's palace we looked across a misty valley to Canton. Since Liberation (everything in modern China dates from Liberation, and you feel that to omit the capital L would be counter-revolutionary and reactionary) the palace has been turned into one of the dullest museums on earth.

These solemn, determined people have developed a frightening flair for dullness and monotony, giving the impression that the ultimate master-plan is for a land fit for zombies to live in.

When the citizens take their families for a Sunday afternoon's outing they trudge stolidly up the spiralling roads to this shabby old palace

(getting their kicks from the thought that this was once forbidden territory), and wander around an unending series of pictures showing the success stories of various conquering comrades. There are pictures of strikes and riots; there are banners and posters, and a glowering line-up of frowning implacable Big Brothers.

Below us was a huge stadium with concrete terraces rising sharply, in tiers, from a patchy field.

"Used to be execution ground," said Sam. "Now is football field."

A group of young footballers in red track suits jogged across the spot where a few thousand dazed wretches once stirred the dust with their death struggles.

"Mostly," Sam said, "they used shoot."

"It's not entirely your dynamic charm—they think you're from Russia."

This, of course, was before Liberation, in those scandalous old days when, if you disagreed with prevailing political opinion you woke up some morning to find your wrists tied behind you and a man doing something to your eyes with a black bandage.

"Where do they execute them now then?" I asked. But there are times when Sam doesn't seem to catch our harsh Australian words. Like now.

In a park where white swans drifted across ornamental lakes we recklessly left our car to look at an old building and were instantly overpowered by a surging shock wave of children.

We had interrupted an out-door kindergarten class and while teacher blew her whistle furiously for order, these usually stolid, unsmiling little mites milled clamorously around us; hugging our knees, clutching our hands, the tiniest ones of all tugging at our ankles.

Riggers and I had fallen instantaneously and hopelessly in love with China's enchanting children long before, but, until this mass demonstration, we had waited in vain for some sign that our affection wasn't an entirely one-sided affair. They all kept shouting one word, over and over.

"Uncles," explained Sam, "they say you're uncles from foreign place."

The two newly-elected uncles gathered up armfuls of

suddenly-acquired nephews and nieces, stroked hands, patted heads, grinned smugly at each other. It was a warm moment in a cold country, and when, at last, the rowdy, reluctant class had been herded away, the tourist route round palace, park, and pagoda seemed to have lost its interest.

Preening ourselves a little on the quiet charm that must have captured the hearts of these discerning children, we told a British business man about our conquest. I shall always hate that guy for what he said.

"They do it all the time; it's all part of the act. And it wasn't uncles those kids were saying. They were saying: 'Men from Soviet Union.' "

Along Canton's ugly waterfront where the ferryboats hoot and wail day and night, 60,000 water folk live out their squalid lives aboard sampans. Packed in tight rows, side by side, these strange captive boats never move out into the river, never feel the stirring of the main tide. Only the slap of the wash from a passing ferry, or a squeak from the mooring lines when the wind changes.

We picked our way along a catwalk between the clutter of floating hovels that mean home to enough people to populate a European city. Tiny babies teetered on the gunwales, ready to topple at any moment and disappear into the muddy swirl; but each child had a

"Taxi! Taxi!"

bundle of wood, like a marker buoy on a mooring, lashed to its shoulders. When they fall in there's almost certain to be some sampan dweller on hand to fish them out with a long bamboo pole, but the danger is that, without their buoys they couldn't be seen in the thick water.

The sampan people on the outer fringes, the ones who can still free their boats from the clogged mass inshore, and who still ply for hire, wanted 30 cents too much to scull us miles downstream to Canton university, so interpreter Sam shook his head and we walked through reeking fish and

rotting vegetables to a ferry jetty.

Looking back at the hideous grey city from midstream, we could see tall, twin spires pointing resolutely through the mist towards heaven.

"Roman Catholic cathedral," said Sam and when we asked him if there were many Catholics in Canton he said promptly:

"Seventeen hundred," then drew our attention away to the grotesque green hulks with towering sterns and multiple decks, that run up the China coast to Shanghai. Now they were lying out in the deep water, waiting for the tide.

As we nosed in towards the university jetty, crews of big, bosomy girls (not by any means the most usual sight in China) went by in racing eights, plugging away doggedly against the hindrance of the stream, and a shouting coach followed them in a speedboat with an outboard motor.

Students at Canton university pay only for their food, the State provides the rest, which consists of red brick barracks, lecture rooms, and vast, beautiful grounds around which we trudged until our feet ached. The students improvise furniture from old boxes and hammocks and reduce their monastic living quarters to cheerful, studious slums.

Every wall, every tree on the campus (how did that American college term persist in a Chinese university?) is plastered with sheets of newspaper. On these sheets the students air their views (with Indian ink and brush), ask questions and criticise (Sam said) the administration.

"Listen, Sam," we said, looking him right in the eye, for we were friends now, and knew him well. "Give it to us straight; you mean these boys and girls exercise complete freedom of thought and speech out here on these sheets? You mean they ask whatever questions they like?"

"Certainly, they're free," Sam said, "in fact they're encouraged to think for themselves and to ask questions."

We picked a sheet at random, and he translated the searching question that was burning a hole in some freeborn student's brain.

"How can I become a better socialist? By striving to achieve political maturity or by specialisation?"

"You see," cried Sam, in modest triumph, "they say just what they like."

"Yeah and the way they say it, everybody likes what they say."

"Please?" Sam was puzzled.

"Skip it," we said.

So that nobody gets any upstage notions of social superiority, everyone in China is asked to do a certain amount of manual labour every week. It is the sort of informal, please-yourself invitation that the United States Government extends to young American males when their draft number comes up and the People's

"Now is that a nice answer to 'What do you like most about your new job?' "

Government has a way of asking such favours that makes the answers highly predictable.

Students interrupt their studies of electronics to go out into the paddy fields and swing a prehistoric hoe; bank managers roll up their pants and go out barefoot to help clean the streets.

Psychologically, as a leveller, it's probably great stuff; economically it doesn't seem to make much sense. This nation, with 70 per cent of its population illiterate and unskilled, has an almost unbelievable dearth of experts. (And this is a place where an expert is a man who knows the reason why a car has gears), yet they waste the expert's precious time swinging a hoe to prove the obvious fallacy that all men are born equal. To us it seemed a crazy setup, a dangerous inhibition that simply added up to snobbery spelt backwards.

Chairman Mao Tse-tung sets the example, and his Ministers get the message with supersonic speed. For three months of the year he goes on into the farms and villages to show the people that he's just a humble peasant like themselves. But no matter how much clay he collects on his boots he remains something of a deity and he isn't noticeably leaning over backwards to

"Like Mao says—it does one good to toil in the fields with one's co-workers."

correct the popular impression that he is only slightly less than supernatural.

The newspapers, when they report how he dropped in casually on a coolie's mud but and sipped tea, do so with a respectful sucking-in of the breath like a British daily gushing the news of Princess Margaret's visit to a coal-miners' canteen. And already there are regular tours to visit Mao's birthplace. In the temples the joss sticks still burn steadily, but China's big torch flames exclusively for Mao.

Whenever the Chairman gets the urge to go back to the land (as he once did when the May Day procession was on in Peking) smart career men in the Government also find themselves yearning for the simple life and start reaching for their mattocks.

It appears to be a ridiculously off-beat way to run a country when you're accustomed to the balanced sanity of our own section of a Western civilisation where a soldier runs the General Post Office, an estate agent runs the Army, a city business man is in charge of primary production, and a farmer is boss of social services.

China's Minister for Fisheries, for example, needs rather more practical qualifications for his job than would his Australian opposite number. Where we come from if the guy has been a faithful party plugger, if he can spell the word "fish" and maybe point in the direction of the sea, he's in. In China the Minister for Fisheries operates, for part of the year, from the deck of a trawler, he sails with the fleets; he trudges the markets; he has scales on his hands; and he reeks. But he knows his job. "I think" said Sam the interpreter one day, "I learn much from you." But Sam wasn't the only one who had been learning things while we'd been together.

There was a vivid pink poster on the wall near our hotel and those who could read were laboriously reading it to those who couldn't. At home it would have been the big news of what prices the bookmakers were offering for Saturday's races but what it said was: "Thrift is glory - waste a crime!"

Like I say, Sam isn't the only one who's learning things.

Through tall, wrought-iron gates, rusty, neglected, and now permanently ajar, an old stone bridge leads across the Pearl River to the International Concession.

There was a time (before Liberation) when bearded and turbanned Sikh sentries stood guard here, ready to bar the way with bayonets to any

Chinese impudent enough to attempt to cross to the sacred soil.

Now a ragged army of bicycles wobbles across, and coolies with unspeakable loads dangling from their bony shoulders, patter by on hard, bare feet.

The raw pylons of a new power line stand on splayed, metallic feet on the balding remains of what were once green velvet lawns.

Among the ruins of the formal gardens, behind corroded railings, and crumbling walls, the stately old homes of the Concession now house hundreds of families.

From mullioned windows washing droops limply over decaying stonework. Cheerful, filthy, entrancingly beautiful, impregnably antibiotic, little children play on dignified doorsteps that have known the pompous tread of ambassadors.

There is garlic in the air.

Suddenly I get a piercing premonition. I have a vision of Riggers and self busily knitting socks in Canton gaol, for Riggers has just whipped out his sketchbook again. In China only spies carry sketchbooks, and the education of every citizen, from creche to crematorium, is aimed at producing a hyper-sensitivity to enemy agents who are generally believed to be planning to launch bacteriological warfare at any moment. Me, I am turning in my badge, my false moustache, and my bottle of invisible ink; there just isn't any future in espionage around here. The last time Riggers did this sketching bit was on the train coming up from Shumchun when he began jotting down the essential characteristics of some secret military installation, like a railway station hamburger stand. His movements were watched with embarrassing interest by what looked like a 17-year-old, four-star general in the People's Army. This character wore an astrakhan fur cap, a shiny, creased khaki uniform, an uncomfortably prominent service revolver, huge gold star-spangled epaulettes and blue-and-white basketball boots. And while Riggers nonchalantly roughed in a few line drawings of our surroundings the general gave us an unblinking look that was so old fashioned that it was practically Ming dynasty.

Along the gravel towpath of the old Concession marches a weird procession. Single file, and out of step, a straggle of youths appears, beating drums, clanging gongs, and brandishing banners on bamboo poles. There is no regular beat to the drums, no marching rhythm; they are just bashing away aimlessly, enjoying the noise, like babies beating toy buckets in a playpen.

Sam says that these are young workers, caught in the glory of China's Forward Leap (in the new China you automatically learn to think in capitals when you're considering matters like the Forward Leap, Rectification, and Liberation) and they are celebrating some new achievement in their work. We look at their faces, hoping to catch some hint of their great inner exultation, the magic of Mao that makes this whole amazing country tick. But every face is blank, expressionless, and we begin to realise what a hopeless task we have taken on in trying to make sense of China in a few short weeks, with our minds incurably hitched to Western ideas. The procession wanders off over the bridge, the

"Oh, no, gentlemen—this parade only for volunteers to work 72 hour week."

banners bob beneath the arch of the gate and the drumming merges with the noises of the river.

Later that same day, about seven in the evening, we saw a bunch of weary workers marching this same single-file, out-of-step way, through the gloom of Canton, to their union meeting.

"What are they after?" we asked Sam. "Shorter hours? More pay?"

Sam's expression was pained, as if we had asked him if these citizens were on their way to apply for migration papers to the United States. No, he said, they are concerned because they feel they aren't doing enough to help the Forward Leap.

One comrade it seemed had just got hold of the novel notion that if they were to cut out their Sunday off each week they would reach their work target a lot quicker. The idea had made quite a hit with the union members so they'd given up their evening's rest to go along to the hall and talk about it. They'll decide to work Sundays all right, but don't think their sacrifices will go unrewarded. Comes Monday lunchbreak and everybody gets to beat a shiny new drum. At this point in the narrative I imagine that keen students of the world scene will be keeping a wary eye on both prose and picture, screening them for signs that the brain-bleaching process has set in. And they may find what they're looking for when I mention that our own alert-and-suspicious phase has passed. I mean the period when we looked through slitted lids at every boiler-suit in case it concealed a security cop; when we cautiously whispered to each other out of range of any wall that could possibly be wired for sound.

Currently our only concern is that there isn't anyone watching over us, for, ever since Sam bowed farewell to us at Canton, we have been crawling across Southern China on a train in which not one single person, except us, speaks English. And the nearest approach to a friend we have on board is a lean, aesthetic party in a peaked cap whose apparent ambition it is to see jasmine tea running out of our ears. He darts into the compartment every few minutes lugging a huge brass kettle, and tops up the thick tea mugs with scalding water.

When this chap is not leaning over with his kettle there's an equally dedicated party with a switch broom; or man with a mop; or a damp rag, investigating rumours that some saboteur of the People's good name has dropped a cigarette butt.

"Just relax and enjoy three days to Peking on the People's Own Train!"

Sharing a four-berth cabin with us is a Chinese business man from Hong Kong, and his twentyish son. Both dressed European style, both behaving exactly as if we weren't present, they are heading for Peking too, and we are stuck with them for two days and three nights. This is not an attractive prospect because papa seems to be in serious training for the world's spitting championship, and, on present form, there doesn't seem to be the slightest danger of the title leaving China. When the chips are down there is little doubt that this wholehearted performer will surpass even his country's greatest expectorations.

With the son we play a non-stop game of radio switch. He switches it on (control of your own switch is one of the big privileges of small compartments) and the walls quiver with the howlings of some hellish oriental choir. (Not all oriental music is hard on western ears; I have heard a Chinese girl singing China Nights in her own language and it sounded more beautiful than any other song I can remember.) When our tortured nerves can take no more punishment we switch it off and glower at him with a touch-that-damn-knob-and-you'll-get-your-block-knocked-off look. He switches it on again and shoots over a you-do-and-I'll-call-that-security-cop-who-just-went-by glare. In the evening there is a truce period. The little guy loves to listen to a comedy show that sounds like a Chinese Amos'n Andy team and has the studio audience rolling in the aisles. Since they seem nice, good natured guys, who don't scream, and yell, and bully, we fold our arms, wish fervently that we could speak Chinese, and restrain our switch itch.

All day, and all night, the train rolls across China pushing steadily northwards through an eternity of paddy fields towards Hankow. Rusty water trickles in orderly channels, and tiny cascades ripple down terraced hillsides, from one geometrical pattern paddy field to another.

Every time we glance out from the window, for as long as the daylight lasts, we see what looks like the same patient man, and the same plodding buffalo, both shin deep in shining mud, guiding a prehistoric plow through the sloppy soil. That man's ancestors, and that buffalo's ancestors probably ploughed this same little plot in this same way a thousand years ago, and it is our guess that the beast is only fractionally less curious about any world beyond the paddy fields than the man.

You see lines of black-clad women, brown-faced beneath their soup-plate hats, paddling through the slough, carefully planting the vivid green rice shoots. Tiny children leading solemn grey buffalo to water; thin, anxious men trotting along the banks between the plots with cruelly heavy baskets sagging at the ends of the straining carrying poles. The scenery never varies; the neat little mud ponds, cut into squares and rectangles, trim as market gardens, stretching away to the horizon. Bent backs never straightening as the train rumbles by. No-one ever looks up, and children don't wave. China is much too busy to be standing around gaping at trains.

If these characters in the coolie hats could be told of a wonderful world of washing machines; tennis gals in gold lace panties; electric blankets; J. Fred Muggs; I-Love-Lucy; Starkweather; and Liberace, I doubt very much whether it would alter their thinking any more than Hans Andersen affects yours and mine. A sick buffalo in the paddy field is far more important locally than a dead dog in a sputnik, and their immediate ambition, the one that they, personally, can do something about, is producing two bowls of rice against last season's one bowl.

The lesson which we are trying to learn by constant repetition, is that comparisons between the China we're seeing now, and the United States, or Britain, or Australia, are hopelessly irrelevant. The only realistic comparison is between old China and new China. We never saw it in the old picturesque pigtail days, but we can't fail to notice that the things that matter to the ordinary people of any land, the top priority things like hospitals, schools, workers' housing blocks, and clinics, are all new.

The first question that any English-speaking Chinese asks a visitor hasn't anything to do with Sun Yat Sen, salt mines, or summits. It is always: "Have you seen the bridge?" We crossed it last night at Hankow and saw the lights proudly outlining each gaunt girder, reflected in the swirling currents of the yellow Yangtze River 100 feet below. At last, after arbitrarily bisecting the country for centuries, the great stream has been spanned, the old maddening detours made unnecessary, and a direct link established between north and south.

Now we are in northern China and the dark blue human flood is in spate all around us. Everyone (except soldiers and police) of every age, and of either sex, wears navy blue military style tunic, and pants. Many wear an engine-driver's cap of the same coarse, hard-wearing duck material. There is no variation in colour, or pattern, never an individual touch. Women look like men, girls look like boys, and frequently both tunic and pants are so heavily padded, quilt-fashion, against the cold, that the wearer becomes entirely shapeless. A modern Chinese, in cool weather, is no longer distinguishable as a person with personal anatomical characteristics, and body movements. He, she, or it, is merely a sexless bundle of navy blue working clothes. It is as though the whole population, conscripted into a huge, unarmed army, had been clothed by the quartermaster's store.

After Hankow the blue swarm almost smothered the train, clogging corridors, and cluttering the over-crowded dining car to suffocation point. For the first time on this tour the people are showing curiosity in the two quaintly-dressed, mysterious Europeans who emerge at meal times. Our appearance in the dining car attracts roughly the same startled attention that a couple of Venusians with suction-cap feet and head antennae might expect. Broad Mongolian faces, previously as blank as Buddha's death mask, suddenly dribble rice as bulging, overfull mouths gape in astonishment at the astounding spectacle of western clothes, and at the harsh sound of western voices. Brown eyes, carelessly rimmed with gravy, peer in amazement over the rice bowls.

As soon as we edge in diffidently through the sliding door, and stand swaying with the others in the crowded aisle, the car attendant dashes forward, somehow finds us seats, then whips off the tablecloth, which is always filthy, and hastily substitutes a new one. Our travelling companions are by no means sophisticated, fastidious city folk, and their table manners are strictly functional, with no Emily Post overtones. When they eat they take their food like a record-attempting aircraft taking on fuel, the idea being to reach capacity within the shortest possible time.

Their chopsticks are a mere blur, and even though they hold the rice bowl against their lower

Truly, you were never lovelier.

lip an invariable 25 per cent of the stuff finishes on the cloth, either by design or accident; by deflection or rejection. But we rate a clean cloth, and the attendant very undemocratically orders the other occupants of the table away, leaving two of us in uncomfortable possession of a table that should seat four. We try hard to explain to him that this doesn't sit well with our western notions of fair play, that we just want to take our turn with everyone else, as we would have to do at home. But it's not good, the only English word he understands is beer, so we say it loud and clear. (For the record, it is good beer.)

Nobody appears to complain about this discrimination, though the car is always crowded, and there is no noticeable resentment. China's traditional good manners towards guests seem to have courteously survived all the social changes.

The menu is in Chinese, Russian, and English, and ordering is simple. We point to the English, the attendant glances across at the Chinese version and nods. When it comes to paying we hold out a fistful of assorted currency and he takes what he needs. But no tip, no ten per cent.

As the long journey drags on we are beginning to look like a pair of singularly unjolly swagmen, with five o'clock shadows that run through a.m. to p.m. The washroom facilities on this train are a little outside our normal experience, and in this respect we are timid travellers. To begin with (and, as far as we're concerned, to end with) no distinction is drawn between the sexes, and though the attendants battle bravely with mops, the standard of hygiene achieved is still considerably lower than that prevailing in public lavatories at overcrowded football grounds at home. We aren't bold enough to lock ourselves in here, to ignore the atmosphere, and endure the constant frenzied hammering on the door long enough to have a shave, so it may well be that when we arrive in Peking the locals may imagine that two new Rasputins have hit town.

There was a bad moment this morning. Lying on my bunk, I was reading a copy of Esquire. The sliding door of our cabin was wide open, and after a few minutes I became aware that someone

"Hey waiter! Where's my crepe suzette?"

was standing there, watching me intently. I looked up to meet the basilisk stare of an enormous Russian (whom we hadn't previously sighted on the train) who was unabashedly reading the turned-over page of my magazine article. I'm not certain, but I fancy that his lips were moving, forming the words as his brain laboriously passed the letters down. Wondering what on earth could have caught his eye so compellingly, I flipped back the page, and felt my scalp tighten. Right across the sheet was an American's sketch of Malenkov, and beneath it the big, bold headline clearly visible at ten paces said WHAT MALENKOV TOLD ME.

Canton is a thousand, and more, monotonous miles south of us now, but in all the time that it has taken us to move, village by village, and town by town, up here to Fungtai,

we have seen no tractor, no truck, no automobile, no mechanisation of any kind, and no artificially-surfaced road.

Every acre, in the countless millions of acres stretching away from our eyes to the very rims of China, has been broken and cultivated by hand, as a western-world suburbanite tames his tiny back garden. Paddy fields have now given way to the widest, flattest farmlands we have ever seen, but there is still the same wonderful land-tidiness. Every ditch is squared as neatly as a concrete drain; every seed row in the crops meticulously straight, and exactly parallel with its neighbour so that it seems that, in all this incredible pastoral precision, there is not one single spadeful of carelessly turned earth. There must be scarcely a handful of Chinese soil that hasn't, at some time, been crumbled between human fingers; scarcely a crumb of it that hasn't been pressed by some patient, plodding human foot.

Without any modern aids at all, without electricity, or gas, or synthetic power of any sort; without gasoline, or oil, or coal; without seeders, reapers, or binders; with nothing but sweat and supernatural determination, these invincible people have brought their whole huge land to bear. With their strong hands they have pushed, and kneaded it into rich productivity.

A family of nine (grandmothers, aunts, daughters-in-law, nieces, nephews) harnessed like animals, hauls a home-made harrow across a boundless field while the driver

from here, at the far end of the history book.

If you want to acquire some faint understanding of China, and the Chinese, as we are trying so hard to do now, I believe you should occasionally forget the belligerent May Day processions swaggering past the benevolent big and little brothers in Tienanmen Square. Forget for a moment the brash

balances barefoot on the rake, using his body weight to force the teeth down into the dark earth.

Along a brown dirt road, between the bright green rows of the young barley and millet, comes a fantastic team. A pony (Shetland size), a mule, and a steer, yoked side by side. dragging a creaking cart with solid wooden wheels. The load they haul would be enough to send a truck gasping into low gear, and their unshod hooves claw desperately at the shining ground, but a bamboo whip flicks inexorably about their ears, and the cart inches slowly forward.

By a neat little mud-walled village set among a grove of thin trees, two men ceaselessly pedal a primitive treadmill, operating a pathetically inadequate water-wheel that lifts, perhaps, a jam-tin full of water at a time, scooping it up and spilling it on the higher level.

Three pig-tailed little girls of doll-playing age, trudge round and round, leaning on a wooden bar, turning a great stone mill wheel. And over the vast farmlands, to the skyline, and far beyond, tiny grey donkeys struggle through the brown dust, pulling ancient, wheel-shaped, stone plows that somehow produce a perfect furrow.

A man and two boys march briskly through a crop spraying against insect pests. The man carries across his shoulders a long bamboo pole from which are hung bags of the precious poison, and as he walks the boys beat these bags with sticks till a white cloud settles over the sprouting grain. Australia, with its aerial crop-dusting teams, and its helicopters hovering over the wheatlands, is an aeon, two aeons, away banners, the rehearsed, word-perfect parrot cries, and even the gilded busts of mighty Mao himself. I believe you should remember this China out here in the farmlands; patient, primeval China where the peasants can neither read nor write. They know nothing of any world beyond the edges of their village; they aren't communists, or capitalists, or any sort 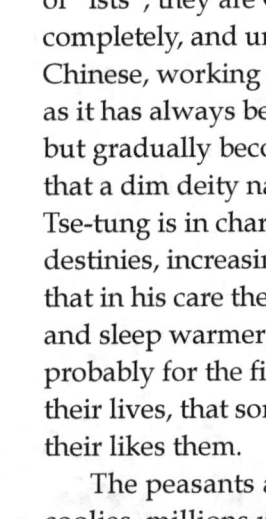 of "ists"; they are Chinese; completely, and unchangeably Chinese, working their land as it has always been worked, but gradually becoming aware that a dim deity named Mao Tse-tung is in charge of their destinies, increasingly conscious that in his care they eat better and sleep warmer; feeling probably for the first time in their lives, that somebody up their likes them.

The peasants and the coolies, millions upon millions of them, are born with the instinct that they are doomed to be pushed around by someone, and it doesn't matter much to them whether a Ming or a Mao does the pushing. What does matter is which big boss puts most rice in the bowl, and, on this score, it is unquestionably Mao first, and the rest nowhere.

Slowly, though, the 4,000-year-old scene is changing.

Intellectuals (in these areas that means people who can read a couple of hundred characters) are being sent out, missionary style, into the villages, to lecture on literacy, birth-control, and, of course, Rectification, and the Forward Leap. To forestall any notions of class distinction the intellectuals sleep on the earthen floor alongside their farmer friends, and rise at dawn to work with them in the fields. It is only when the daylight is gone that the lectures begin. As far as we can see right now it is this earnest, hardworking, can't-waste-a-minute China that will emerge and endure.

PEKING:

When we left Canton, three nights, two days, and 1,500 miles ago they told us "You will arrive Peking at 7.22 a.m.," and we grinned to ourselves a little at the pompous precision of it, but that's exactly how it was, 7.22 right on the minute.

Hu Er Chien, the young Intourist man, was waiting there on the long, chilly platform to meet us, to find us a taxi and deliver us to the Hsinchiao hotel over by the great Chunkgwemen gate to the old walled city. In this, the capital of Red China, the place where the omnipotent Mao Tse-tung and the urbane Chou En-lai live; where every man, woman and child wears coarse, navy blue uniforms, as alike as convicts in a vast gaol, we expected that the cold shadow of communism would at last fall over us.

From now on, we were certain that our every word and movement would be watched and recorded, and that the water colours on the walls of our room would hide a microphone. Europeans whom we met later (people who live and work in Peking for various reasons) told us that this is almost certainly what did happen; that the names of the cafes we ate in, of the people we talked to, and the shops we visited would all be recorded, somewhere, in minute detail. Somewhere there would be a fat dossier of reports from the pedicab men who rode us around; from the room boys at the hotel; from the switchboard girls; cab drivers; and cafe proprietors. That's what the old hands told us; but if there was any supervision it must have been subtle, for, though we were instinctively alert, we never detected any attempt to monitor our movements, and there was definitely none to restrict them.

Hu Er Chien explained that this was one of his busy days, wrote his phone number on a card in case we needed him, excused himself, and left us to tackle the big new city our own way.

Riggers and I have long ago developed a formula for new towns. The first day we always walk everywhere; no cabs, no buses, no trams. This way we can feel the city, hear its own special noises, smell the smells, and sense its mood. This way you can make friends with a place. So now we wandered along sad, shabby streets that may once have been gay boulevards, window shopping in shops as pathetic as those of a goldfields ghost town, staring at shoddy merchandise, and primitive window displays. It was like walking through the movie lots at 20th Century Fox and coming across a set made ready for a scene from some long-forgotten era. The sidewalks, flanking broad streets, may once have been paved and clean, but now they are just worn tracks, bumpy and uneven, and the grit swirls up with every shuffling footfall.

Pursued by pedicab men, who rode beside us urging us to take advantage of their command of English and their cheap rates, we went by the high stone walls of Legation Row, where the embassies are, with their national flags, their brass plates and their Chinese sentries. We found Marco Polo street, and followed it to the shopping centre they used to call Morrison-street but which the Chinese call Wanfuching. We wandered through dingy little bookshops, taking books down from the shelves, in the English section, reading a modern Chinese history explaining how Russian might brought about the final defeat

Temple of Heaven

"Keep your engine running pal—we might need you in a hurry!"

of Japan in world war II. There was no mention of America, or the atom bombs of Hiroshima and Nagasaki. There were books there by Scotland's traitor Royal Marine Andrew Condron and his twelve American companions in shame who changed sides in Korea; and by New Zealand's Rewi Alley who has lived, these many years, at the Peking Hotel.

We tried to see Alley, but the message came down that he was unavailable, that he was out of town, and wouldn't be back in time to meet us. We stared at the movie posters; a story of a basketball hero, a story of Russia's security triumphs over a foreign spy ring; and a dozen other stories we couldn't work out. Homogenous navy blue citizens went by, never giving us a passing look, none differing from the other by so much as a coloured necktie or a head scarf.

In a grassless little park where boys scuffled around a football the dust billowed as thick as a morning mist.

An enthusiastic lover of Peking (his memories mercifully blurred by nostalgia for another Peking that must have been buried back in 1949) had told me that this, with Athens, was the most beautiful city in the world. All the way from Shumchun the picture was with us of a gracious, warm city, alive with colour and sunlight, and green with the trees without which no city is really beautiful. It was a picture that had sustained us through the grim poverty of rural China, and through the minor miseries of an overlong train trip.

Now we were in a Peking where every faded house and shopfront pleaded for paint; a gritty, grey place where the skeletons of young trees on the edges of the dusty streets only emphasised the sadness. We are accustomed to the opulence of jostling traffic; to red buses, and green streetcars, two-tone automobiles; neon signs; and the gay kaleidoscope of western clothes. To us, on that first day, Peking was like a glimpse of Limbo.

Whatever this city may have been, she now is like a once lovely and lovable woman who has got past caring about her looks. A woman who hasn't bothered about lipstick, or hairdressers for more years than she can recall. A woman grown apathetic, or eccentric to the point where beauty is no longer important, if it is even remembered.

When you're a visiting Pressman in this town you get the tipoff, pretty soon, that your presence is required at the Ministry of Foreign Affairs. We went, by cab, through bicycle-cluttered streets, driving American-style on the right-hand side of the road, with the driver keeping a thumb pressed almost incessantly on the horn. At first we thought that was a personalised, high-pressure deal, especially for us; the frantic news hawks being rushed to their appointment with the top tunics of the People's Propaganda section; but it turned out that everybody here drives this way.

Peking must be easily the world's noisiest city; everyone makes and sustains a noise of some kind. Cab drivers toot on high-pitched, fierce-volume tooters; triumphant workers beat drums and gongs; mourners explode firecrackers; pedlars blow bugles; firetrucks wail; trains whistle; loud-speakers bellow on every street corner; and two million bicycle bells ring without pause. I remember once doing an interview with mouth-organist Larry Adler when he suddenly sprang up and ran because someone had started up a vacuum-cleaner and the pitch of its whine was physical pain to his sensitive ears. A fellow like Adler could die the death of a thousand decibels in the big-scale bedlam of Peking.

The taxi swung suddenly out of the main street, turning suicidally across the bows of a shrieking Czechoslovakian bus, hooted a piercing rejoinder, then plunged down an alleyway where big-eyed children flattened themselves against tall adobe walls as we passed, and overladen pedicabs edged over on the cobblestones to let us scrape precariously by. We saw all this only in swift, shutter-like glimpses, because, like anyone who has ever driven a car, we were gauging the width of the lane, and the spread of the ear's wings. We kept spotting nasty angular corners ahead; knots of wobbling cyclists; pedicabs and hundreds of tottering babies playing in the dangerous dust and our eyes were closed most of the time, as we murmured desperate impromptu prayers. At last the gear-mangling ceased and we were stationary.

Through heavy double doors in a thick wall, past a cold-eyed sentry with a huge, shiny holster, in to a pleasant, garden-green courtyard, to the steps of an imposing building. Collonades, archways, and wide flights of stone stairs. It could have been the Transylvanian embassy back in the good old days. Across the sort of entrance hall peculiar to embassies, and Hollywood movies, into a vast, overawing reception room.

We sat on the edges of plum-coloured, early Victorian plush chairs, peering about us in a state of tension which was about half dentist's waiting-room, half headmaster's study, staring at the distant, decorated ceiling, and the big, brass-tubed chandeliers. As we waited we murmured to each other in voices so low that the words were lost, we both became taut with our own apprehensions and when the door opened we jumped as if we'd been caught planting time bombs.

Madame Chen Hsui Hsia, and a man whose name we made out merely as Ho, came in with gracious smiles and outstretched hands. Jasmine tea was served, and we got down to business. Madame Chen is a middleaged, pleasant-faced woman, with a gentle manner, and a quick smile. At home she would be the friendly, understanding boss of the little schoolhouse or the president of the Parish Mothers' Committee. She wore the usual military-type navy blue tunic, but hers was of serge, and her slacks were pressed to a knife-edge crease. Ho was simply a scholarly-looking man in blue with glasses and with a good knowledge of English.

What were our main interests? they wanted to know, could they help us in any way?

"I think," said Madame Chen in her soft voice, "It is very significant that your people should want to know about China, that your paper should have sent you here." All four of us quickly relaxed, and chatted easily. We tried hard to define our catch-as-catch-can methods of working as a cartoonist-writer team, explaining how we play our countries by ear and how we would be more likely to find our material in free wanderings around the alleyways and the markets than in conducted tours of factories and plants. Madame Chen nodded understandingly. "Just let us know, when you're ready, if there's anything special you want to see and we'll try to arrange it for you."

They issued us with impressive scarlet gold-lettered press passes (on which the only piece of English was our names), complete with passport pictures, and with forms to fill

"Y'know, all this waiting is psychological stuff—it's supposed to make us feel small."

out for any special interview requests.

"Who you like to see?" asked the forms, "What you like talk about?"

We said we'd like to find our way around for a few days, ride a few pedicabs, buy a few things in the shops, making a little sense out of the strange big grey city in the way that we have tackled so many other cities, and then maybe we'd have questions. So we shook hands all round and smilingly left it at that.

. . . THE FORBIDDEN CITY

Immediately outside the Hsinchiao hotel, where we live, lurks a line-up of some of the most villainous-looking characters on earth. These are pedicab men and any one of them could confidently stroll into any movie casting department and walk out with a fat Fu Manchu part.

Under the old regime (a heavy-duty phrase around a town grown prim and priggish with five-starry-eyed reform) these homely parties may well have been just what they look like, but now they are strictly bike-pushing Boy Scouts with an honesty bias that is scarcely human.

When the top people of the People's Republic took on the staggering task of making over the medieval madhouse of China, they plainly realised that they weren't going to do it with feather dusters, and I suspect that unlettered citizens such as the pedicabbies, learned about Rectification the rough way. But, whether by magic wand, or rubber truncheon, or a balanced blend of both, honesty has become strikingly prevalent, if not popular, all along the cab ranks.

In any other big city of our experience the sight of two camera-carrying strangers squelching round town in suede shoes brings the clipper crews running to action stations. Begging bowls rattle like machine-gun fire; hands clutch at sleeves, and voices from just below shoulder level mutter murky invitations to blue movies, and off-limits love. Here the pedicab boys were the only ones who approached us.

A pedicab? well, it's a bit like a very ancient wheelchair, that hasn't been oiled since Liberation, hitched on to a slightly older, squeakier bicycle.

"Go 'way! We wanna go for a walk!"

For two yuan you can loll back and make like a Roman Emperor returning from the wars.

"I number 18," confided the least terrifying of the lineup, pedalling steadily alongside us, "Speak English very good, show you city, very cheap," and then he tossed in the type of screwball remark that sends the western mind reeling. "I number one." But we old walkabouters are smart cookies; we haven't spent days kicking around with the Kowloon double-talk set for nothing, we know what the guy means. His official number is 18, but as a guide, interpreter, and Peking pal, he is so far ahead of any possible competition that he must be modestly regarded as number one, the best.

So number 18 and his offsider (Charlie Chan in a dark blue baseball cap and padded cocktail jacket in the same fashionable shade) bore down bravely on twisted pedals and muscled us along a wonderful, enormously wide boulevard to the Tienanmen Gate which is the southern entrance to the Forbidden City. And, after a few blocks, there began to appear on number 18's face that everything-happens-to-me look as he struggled against the dragging weight of Rigger's 200lbs, while number 10 skimmed along, gloating over my puny 160.

They left us on a hump-backed marble bridge over a tributary of the moat that surrounds the entire Forbidden City, and rode away to meet us, hours later, at the northern exit, Shunmenwen, the Gate of Heavenly Prowess. Here, at last, was Peking's beauty.

We went in through a huge, echoing archway in an 80ft. wall salmon-pink with morning sunlight, and the whole dream sequence of the Imperial Palace stretched before us in a mile-long series of cobble-stone courtyards; sweeping, stone staircases, guarded by dragons and griffins and heraldic lions; and archways below towers and temples. Only it isn't the Imperial Palace any more, it's the Working People's Cultural Palace. China clubs its citizens over the head with culture and nonchalant peasants play draughts beneath the gnarled and twisted trees where the Imperial concubines used to sip jasmine tea. Roly-poly children, padded to the chin, bounce a

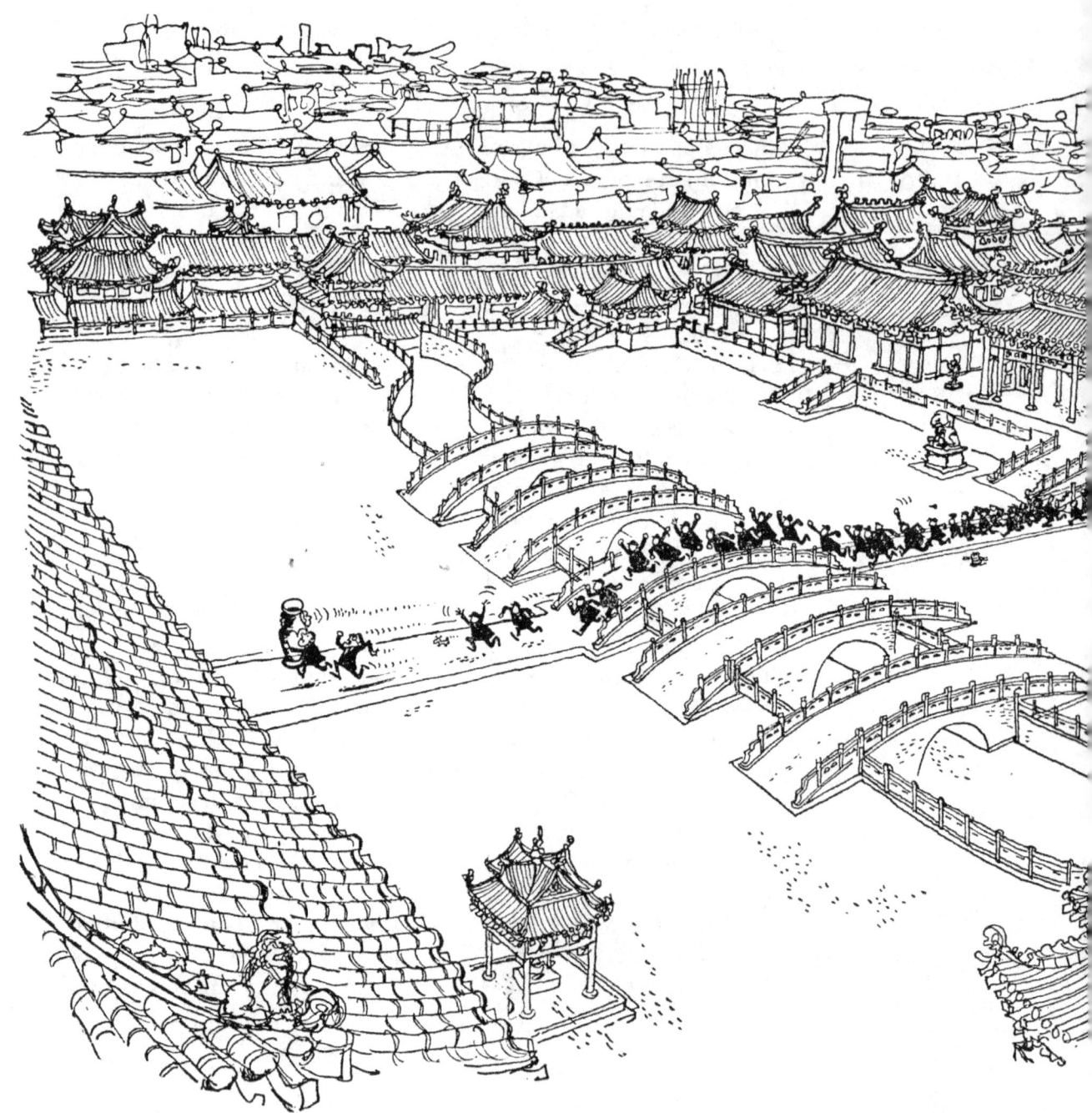

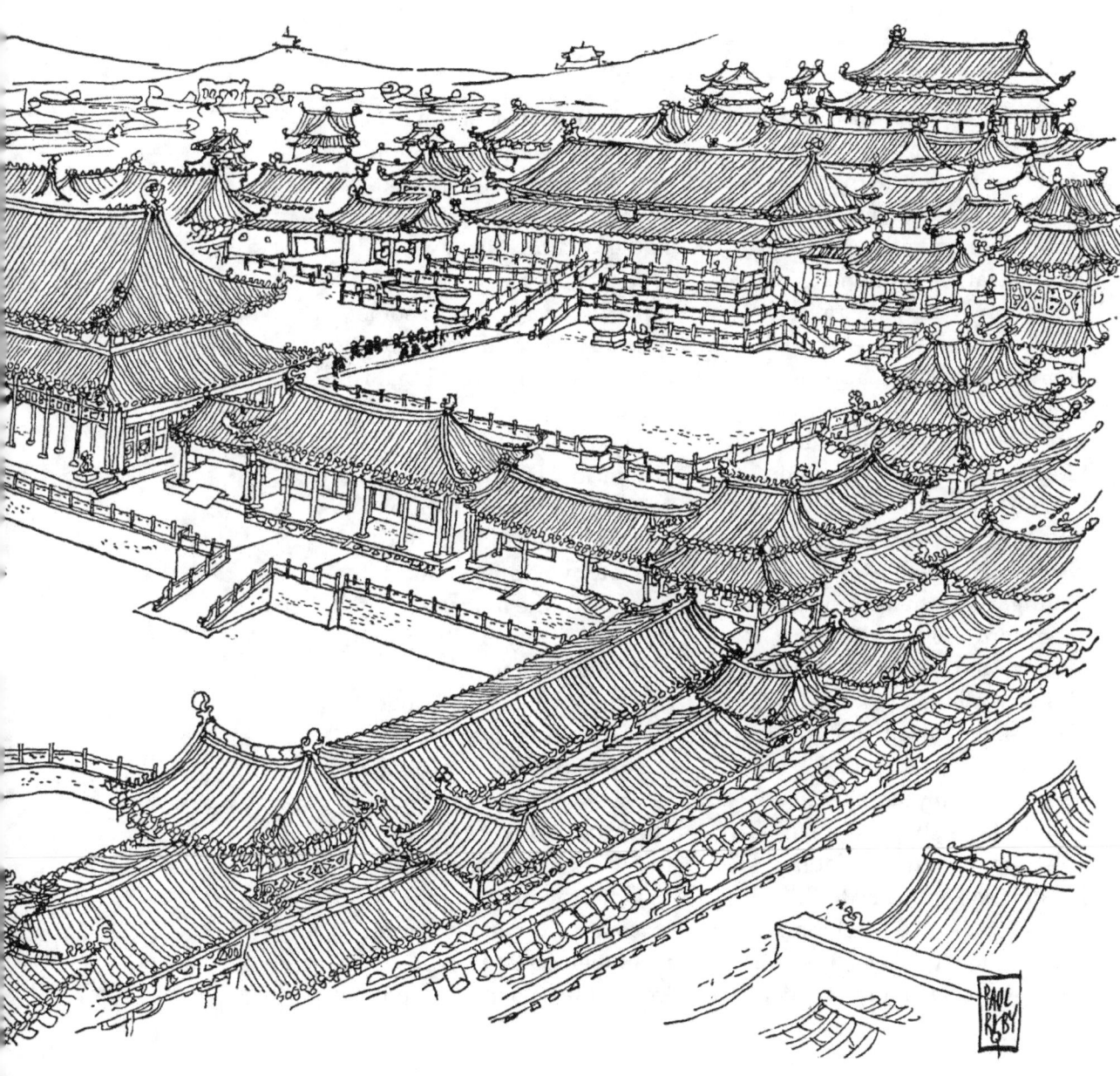

"That's great—causing a disturbance at the Gates of Supreme Harmony!"

ball on the sacred strip where once it was death for anyone but the emperor to tread.

One of the main halls you meet up with early is the Hall of Supreme Harmony where the present day harmony-hunters boost harmonious international relations with exhibitions such as The Movement to Resist American Aggression. There are exhibitions plugging the achievements of Russia, Rumania, Czechoslovakia, Hungary, Vietnam, East Germany, Poland, Bulgaria, Korea, and Indonesia. Never a kind word for the wicked West. But come to think of it have you ever seen a Red China exhibition in your hometown?

There is always a small floating foreign population in Peking and the sixth floor of the Hsinchiao hotel is an international village. It's called the Swedish bar and for about seven shillings you can eat not-so-good caviare to satiation, and drink reasonably good champagne at ten shillings a bottle. At lunchtime, when the villagers drop in for a game of billiards, or a beer, and some European food, there is hardly a country in the world that isn't represented.

Like all villages it is chronically sibilant with rumours, and, as a natural reaction against the monastic monotony of this unnaturally moral city, the first avid question always is: "Know any good juicy scandal?"

"See that guy over there? He's a deserter from the Australian Korean contingent. Always eats alone, seldom speaks to anybody, never to Europeans. Assisted in the interrogation of Allied prisoners-of-war. They used to sit them naked, on blocks of ice, and this chap used to pour

Legation Street —

water over them to help them along with their answers."

It didn't make much sense to me, for the known Allied deserters (one Scottish Royal Marine, and about a dozen Americans, including a few Negroes) are by no means men of mystery. Everyone knows that they live in a dormitory out at Peking university where they are like lost souls in purgatory trying to kid themselves that they've found heaven.

I thought maybe I'd talk to this fellow-countryman of mine, but right away fingers flew to lips, and warning frowns scowled danger signals. In this country a foreign journalist who steps out of line can confidently expect some unhappy hiatus in his writing career, and seeking off-the-cuff interviews with mysterious English-speaking characters is quite a bit too far out of line.

But I could do a little discreet cross-checking so I asked another villager about this Australian.

"Him? Oh he's a doctor from Melbourne with a fast-growing malignant bone disease, and he's here because Peking has the only doctor in the world who knows the answer to it."

The Swedish bar, and its restaurant, is always packed with Russians, Poles, Indians, Swedes, Britons, Frenchmen, and even Portuguese. Delegations of beefy, blond East Germans stamp in like storm troopers, sit down in unison, and eat, it seems, by numbers, while their young, pink-faced leader harangues them, from the top of the table. Salesmen from all countries come, doggedly peddling a line of goods to some of the world's toughest sales-resistance groups.

Instinctively, and invariably, we split into sympathetic camps, the British, the Swedes, the Danes, the French, and all the non-communists gather together; the nordics all so alike in looks, tastes, and behaviour that you can't separate them until you hear them speak. Russians, genial big brothers to all Communists, but never actually mingling with anyone, their ponderous, square-shouldered, heavy-

School Bus —

hipped women striding along corridors in expensive double-breasted trench coats, aloof and self important. We look at them and a sudden ice-dagger of thought pierces our minds with the horrible notion that one day Russia could become a Muscovite matriachy ruled by these fearsome females. It is a thought that makes Khrushchev's Kremlin seem almost benevolent.

Every lunchtime two vital, vigorous young Czechoslovakians come bounding in to drink beer, and eat their lunch with enormous zest. These are most happy fellas. They have just sold the Chinese Government a crematorium; and right now they're flat out supervising its daily operations. For them it has been a good trip, with a nice sale, and good prospects of unloading a lot more of their macabre merchandise.

With the two polished immaculate Swedes who flew in over the polar route, things haven't gone quite so well. They're selling a complete hardboard factory, and though it now begins to look as if they've swung the deal, negotiations have dragged on for so long that their expenses have drifted into brackets which have little relation to the profit on the sale. Cables alone have cost them more than $1000 and they have spent 95 hours sitting-in on 35 conferences devoted, not to the technical problems on which they are topline experts, but to the maddening fine-print of the contract. Now comes a snag; China wants to pay off in goods, not cash, and that's had because it's hard to think of anything that China produces that the western world doesn't produce bigger, better, and faster. And these are unspecified goods. So the conferences start all over again.

A British engineer, here to sell free-piston engines, has been in Peking three months lecturing to universities and eager audiences everywhere, running his movies, talking to trade committees, doing everything but sell. China needs what he's offering, but there are more strings to the deal than there are whiskers in a Peking Opera villain's beard. The engineer must guarantee that an all-British ship will carry the engines, he must state the nationality of the skipper, and of the crew (one American in the fo'csle could atom-bomb the whole contract) and guarantee that the ship won't start from, touch at, or divert to an American port.

It is a strange experience for British subjects (which, of course, all Australians are) to find some corner of a foreign field where somebody rates lower on the popularity poll than the British. If ever President Eisenhower feels the need of ego-equating on account of all those I-Like-Ike badge-bearers, he might do worse than think about Red China. Up here among 600,000,000 simple, earnest folk, he rates just slightly below the Asian flu germ.

From our huge, room-width window we look out at night on to a struggling, dusty little park caught in the angle of two converging streets in the shadows of the city wall. Emaciated trees are shivering in the nakedness of winter though the new green leaves are only a few days away now. From this height we can see across the inner city and over the sprawling suburbs beyond it, but it is hard to believe that this is a capital with 3,000,000

"Aw, heck, I'm going to take mine off and risk the American germ warfare!"

inhabitants for it is as sparsely lit as a shanty town.

Figures crossing the park are indistinct silhouettes; perhaps thirty of them, in the usual haphazard single file, wandering off to some meeting or other, clanging gongs and thumping a listless drumbeat, each face startlingly white with the gauze mask which is fashionable facewear all over

China. Ever since we crossed the railway bridge at Shumchun and saw the first of these masks we have been trying to find out what they're for. But the vagueness that clouds many a simple issue in these mystic parts comes down like a San Francisco fog. Let me give you some grab sample replies; maybe you can figure it out for yourself.

An English-speaking Chinese explained that people suffering from the common cold feel a heavy responsibility to make sure that not through them shall the germ be passed on to weaken China's mighty work force and thus hinder the Forward Leap. This is a view that can be recommended to western folk who take their colds to the office with them as a badge of suffering and sneeze all the way home in the bus and pass the cold on as if it were the Olympic Torch.

Sam, our Cantonese interpreter, said that the mask was simply another example of China's dramatic realisation of the importance of hygiene. He pointed out (and he was dead right) that everybody you see serving or handling food here wears a surgeon's mask. But one of Peking's elder foreign residents (a character wiser than a tree full of owls) claimed that it all started when the People's propaganda mills first began churning out thought-germs about American bacteriological warfare. The ordinary Chinese believes that his country was bombarded with bacteria just as surely as he believes in the seasons.

Children sagging in sacks on their mothers' backs wear masks, so do the stern young sentries keeping watch over every bridge in the land; so do the traffic policemen, and the stunted little girls who drive the elevators. And the dust eternally swirling in from the Gobi desert makes sense of it all.

We have watched these traffic police in action, alert for any hint of bullying, or standover stuff. And you don't have to wait long to see someone break the law by running a light, or ignoring a signal. When this happens the bawling out sounds like a mild reproof compared with the cataclysmic wrath of a New York or Australian cop, and the culprit doesn't look as if he expected to hear the tramp of heavy boots in the night and the dreaded knock of the secret police on the door.

He acts much the same way as any western wrongdoer, with a mixture of embarrassment and defiance, an awkward attempt to keep face with the spectators, without antagonising the law too much. Amateur interpreters have given us some bizarre translations of these exchanges, with the cop saying "Excuse my mentioning it, comrade, but it seems to me you acted somewhat irresponsibly," and the wrong-way cyclist answering with "What you say is a just criticism, comrade." We can't speak Chinese so we wouldn't know about that, but you soon learn to accept hit-or-miss translations with a certain amount of reserve in all the areas inside the Great Wall.

AT DAWN on a grey morning, three incredible days ago, a sudden bugle call, shrill as cockcrow, menacing as a midnight phone call, went echoing round the city walls, and the People's Republic of China declared war. Men, women and children sprang to action stations instantly. There was no confusion, every citizen knew exactly what he had to do and no one was too old or too young to take part.

From every rooftop and lookout post in all Peking a horrible, inhuman bedlam broke out. Brass gongs jarred the senses with flat shivers of sound; cymbals clashed off-key; whistles screamed; firecrackers exploded; drums boomed; and somewhere down among the brave little trees of our park a loudspeaker smashed out a Russian march. And as soon as the last truculent note ebbed

the domineering voice of one of China's merciless radio shrews began nagging at the obedient citizenry. The Government's great anti-sparrow campaign had begun.

China is forever prodding its citizens into some highly organised, all-join-hands campaign or other against mice, or mosquitoes, or flies, or cockroaches. I suspect, though, that mastermind Mao is much more interested in men than

"Reactionary!"

"Quick! There goes another one!"

in mice; that these concerted, communal efforts owe more to psychology than to hygiene; and are planned largely as morale-tighteners and useful exercises in mass discipline.

Right now sparrows have twittered their way to top spot on the hate parade, and all three million of Peking's population have been swiftly mobilised with comprehensive efficiency, to perform terrifyingly absurd tasks. Old men and little children are manning massive walls; clerks are balancing precariously on the shiny, ceramic roofs of temples; housewives are swaying in brittle tree tops, all waving flags on bamboo poles, or else adding in some way to the maddening din. Every twenty yards, along every street and lane, someone rattles a tin, or wields a clapper. Scarecrows dangle from every chimney pot, looking horribly like corpses on a gallows.

Some unknown genius, some modest hero of the Forward Leap, has discovered that a sparrow's flying endurance is two hours maximum, and has come up with the kind of thought that just won't fit readily into the grooves of a western mind. He figures that if enough people make enough noise and wave enough flags then China's sparrows will be forced to remain airborne until they succumb to some form of sparrowish metal-fatigue, or fall exhausted from the skies.

It is a highly significant pointer to the mood and mentality of the new China that the whole country, without criticism or question, has thrown itself fanatically into this crackpotted, do-it-the-hard-way fantasy. These well-drilled people are perfect raw material for May Day marchers, ARP wardens, or storm troops; a stockpile of co-ordinated human energy ready to respond to the lightest touch of Chairman Mao's thumb on the button.

Even the dignified embassies, behind the tall walls of the Legation area, have shouting, clanging, dark-blue figures clambering recklessly over the tiles. All except the Indians, who refuse to take any sort of life in any sort of cause, and the tender-hearted Burmese who have built special bird sanctuaries for any feathered-refugee who flutters over the wall seeking asylum. The British, who traditionally shoot everything that moves in field and wood, are blasting away happily, hanging up record sparrow bags, and proving that the shotgun is mightier than a flag on a bamboo stick, even if the flag is red. In the drawing rooms below, scandalised diplomats wait apprehensively for some rooftop coolie to come down with a case of shotgun pellets in the pants and trigger an international incident.

At the huge, modern hospital across the way surgeons in masks and gowns are methodically beating a privet hedge where a weary sparrow is rumoured to be resting up, plotting new attacks on the Republic. Six floors above, vigorous little uniformed nurses race perilously along narrow balustrades, flicking their banners at the foe.

As a gesture of international goodwill, or maybe because we were half hypnotised by the prevailing padded-cell atmosphere, Riggers and I went out on to the flat roof of the Hsinchiao, took up a couple of spare flags and waved away like crazy until a passing sparrow gave us the sort of look that Caesar gave Brutus when he noticed that his old chum was about to stab him in the sacro-iliac.

All day long the radio vans tour the city so that the little wireless witches can shriek the latest sparrow casualty lists, while the populace cheers as wildly as a Trafalgar Square VE-day crowd. One stubborn sparrow colony remains doggedly entrenched under the

moss-grown slats of the roof of the old gate-house until the fire brigade enters dramatically with sirens wailing and bells ringing. Up shoots a 90-foot extension ladder with an intrepid fireman encaged on the topmost rung. In a few seconds a fierce jet of water ruffles the ancient roof, and as the bedraggled little birds tumble out, wings flapping feebly, a thunderous roar of triumph goes up from the thousand-strong crowd which has gathered around the foot of the ladder.

At midnight of the third deafening day the bird blitz is over. We wake, expecting to hear, from three-day habit, the dreaded din. But over the whole city a beautiful stillness reigns. The gongs, the drums, the whistles are silent. In all Peking there is no sound . . . except for the invincible chirping of the sparrows.

THE HEADLAMPS of our jeep pushed a wedge of light ahead of us through the sinister little alleyways, flicked swiftly over a blue-clad cyclist hunched over his handlebars, caught the gleam of jungle eyes as one of Peking's few cats slunk towards the shadows, and raced along high walls until they rested on green canal water below the city's northern gate.

John Morgan (second secretary to the British Legation) who jeeps nonchalantly around these meandering, one-car-width lanes like Fangio doing a Mille Miglia circuit, had brought us here, quivering, complaining, and pressing our feet hard on imaginary brakes all the way.

The houses along the canal are so old that they seem to lean towards each other for support. Coarse grass sprouts up between the roofing slats, and we had to bend our heads, and hunch our shoulders to squeeze through the doorway of the cafe. Up a flight of twisting stairs, worn to splinters by the feet of people long since dead, and into a smoky, low-ceilinged room where there were just two tables and a huge, ancient glowing stove.

This is Peking's last Mongolian restaurant, and, in more than four centuries, it hasn't bothered to print a menu because every night in all those 400 years the food has been the same, cooked the same way, on that same stove.

It came as no surprise at all when John told us that the camel drivers coming down to China through the mountain pass used to stop by here to grab a fast snack, because, for some reason or other, I've always imagined a camel-driver to be a very low-score gourmet, and the stuff they serve in this place is exactly my idea of camel-driver type food.

The first course is eggs with a difference. The script says that these eggs are 100 years old, and though John, the surefooted old Pekingese, scoffs at this as tourist talk, I believe every word of it. In fact, if I'd had to hazard a swift guess at their age I would have said that the hen that laid those eggs was alive about the same time as Sinanthropus Pekinensis, the famous Peking Man, 500,000 years ago.

Hey, housewives, wanna surprise hubby with a piquant dish that he's never had before? (Unless, of course, you happen to be married to a Mongolian camel-driver.) Put this recipe

"You like more hundred-year-old egg and toasted cockroach, Comrade?"

down in your cook book. Then burn it. The cook book I mean. Take one clutch of eggs (the book calls for fresh ones but when you think what's going to happen to them, does this really matter?); bury them about one foot below the earth surface, in lime; leave to ferment and jell for about 100 years, have your grandchildren dig them up, shell them, slice lengthways then serve. Just one such serve hits the unaccustomed palate like a Lew Hoad serve hitting a gravel court and is apt to leave the victim with a very low opinion of Mongolian wine-and-food societies.

Personally I am something of a faddist about eggs. I don't care for them to be fighting out a photo finish with pteradactyl eggs for age, and I think that cooking them for a century is 99 years 30 days, 23 hours, and 56½ minutes too long. It makes them go black as onyx, and taste like cloudy ammonia poured over crepe rubber.

If, by some freak of physical endurance, the customers are still interested in food after these testing hors d'oeuvres there is another course. Forced to choose between animal, vegetable, and mineral I'd go for vegetable, with a strong suspicion of seaweed. Chopped into a sort of rissole, and slapped on the red-hot iron plate of the old stove, it's fried in pork fat, then heaped into bowls. You eat it (if you're really determined to go through with this reckless experiment, no matter what) with chopsticks. And that, as far as I'm concerned, does it. From my corner a white paper napkin comes fluttering in, signifying that a good, game lad has reached the end of his resources.

Chopsticks are the perfect expression of China's age-old

passion for doing everything the hard way. Old timers will tell you that they are a great aid to digestion, because they compel greedy guys to take on their food in small quantities; but, old timers will tell you anything. They will tell you that Peking is Paris; and we met a British resident in Canton who, sitting in a cafe as squalid as an aborigines'

camp said: "This must seem like civilisation to you chaps after Australia?" (To this we made an Empire-sundering reply which has no place in this report.)

I have made a careful study of chopstick technique all the way through the Far East (which isn't so far at all. To us it's very near) and the really top performers shovel the stuff in at a speed well within dyspeptic range. Their sticks blur like the blades of a cake-mixer; food splatters their faces, the tablecloth, and even an occasional innocent bystander. I wish that, as part of the Forward Leap, China would chop out the chopsticks. The spoon, and the fork are vastly superior weapons.

PEKING:

Undoubtedly the most mixed-up men in this place, at this time, are some visiting Yorkshire miners, here on a union-sponsored package-deal walk into paradise. Into the promised land where it's every man for the State instead of every man for himself. They have been in town only one day, but already puzzled frowns trace the passage of startling new thoughts through sturdy, commonsense Yorkshire minds.

By day they are discovering that all their homebred notions of socialism are spelled backwards in this crazy climate where work is the opiate of the people, and where any man who dared to mention a 35-hour week would qualify for some rugged re-education from his enthusiastic, 60-hour comrades. By night (when western workers are entitled to a few beers in the pub or a few leers in a cabaret) they're bumping disappointedly into the total shutdown on gaiety in this solemn city. Gaiety is anti-revolutionary and reactionary. If, at the end of your working day, you still have enough energy and zest left for night life then, obviously, you have been loafing and failing to give your all for the Forward Leap. Unless there is some dramatic and totally unforeseeable change in the thinking of east and west, then the workers of the world are never going to unite because, right now, they are marching with almost equal determination, in completely opposite directions. The late J. Pierpont Morgan and a street-corner shoe-shine urchin had much more in common, economically and idealistically than has any western worker with this Chinese counterpart.

A good Chinese union man never speaks (and probably never thinks) of matters like better wages, better conditions, shorter hours, and tea breaks. What the talk is about when the wage-slaves get together is how to increase production, step up their output and do more to help China's struggle towards the stars. At union meetings workers get up to denounce themselves as slackers and to promise more effort in future. Every union sets itself some near-impossible work target, and when the impossible has been achieved, proudly turns its shining face once more to the sweaty summits.

On the honest Yorkshire countenances there is beginning to appear a strange, faraway look; the sort of look a man might wear if he were trying to imagine some fervent labor leader attempting to sell China's work ideology to a mass meeting at a Yorkshire pithead.

Shanghai factory workers have pledged themselves to overtake Britain's tyre output within four years, and they're going about it like Vladimir Kuts going after an Olympic gold medal. With disregard for human frailties; struggling beyond exhaustion point; training their hearts and muscles to accept brutal overloads.

When they do finally reach their goal (as they inevitably will) they'll troop around the block beating drums and carrying banners until some sharp-thinking comrade will earn praise and popularity by pointing out that one turn around the block represents the loss of one tyre's worth of work to the People; then everyone will scurry back to his bench, desperate to catch up on the backlog of wasted minutes.

Many times in history great nations have been fanatically dedicated to conquest, or religious reform, but has any nation on this astonishing old earth ever before gone completely overboard on the idea of work? Everyone is obsessed with the Forward Leap . . . and that's precisely what they're doing, they're leaping, progressing from medievalism to modernity, not in the usual leisurely shuffle of centuries, but in huge, impatient bounds. The People's Republic is young (61% of China's population is under 30 years of age) and it just can't wait to get on with

"Now who'd have thought it'd turn out to be THAT sort of union meeting?"

all its staggering, challenging tasks.

Something, some elusive, intangible thing, has set fire to the minds of the Chinese people, literates and illiterates alike, setting them crackling with flames of pride and patriotism. We gaze at all, sometimes in wonder, less and less with ridicule, and often with open admiration; for, whether we like it or not, no sensible observer can fail to realise that this New Deal is the nearest that these wonderful people ever got to a square deal.

CHING LUNG CHIAO:

On the plain the morning heat had been prickly with the restless dust of the Gobi desert, but here where the Great Wall reels and staggers over the Pataling hills, the mountain air was cool and sweet.

The road out from the city to the Yenshan ranges is smooth at first, but soon crumbles into a bumpy 40-mile dirt track with sweaty repair gangs swarming over it; a hundred picks flailing the old worn track. Along the verges, constantly bullied by the bark of our horn, plodded a never-ending procession of donkey carts. Small, shaggy grey donkeys digging sharp little hooves into the dust, hauling mountainous loads, on top of which, as often as not, their ragged masters sprawled in sleep.

There was no other traffic on the road, just one kahki coloured Polish car with suspect shock absorbers and 10,000 donkey carts, until gradually the steepness of the ascent thinned out even these. Now the trail spiralled round and round the contours of the hills. White blossom, like stubborn snow refusing to yield to spring, clung to the almost vertical mountainsides. Tiny, mud-walled houses huddled together for protection in the coils of the road; and always over yard, and pig-sty, and moss-grown roof was the spilling beauty of wild plum blossom, of peach, and of cherry. On walls that may have stood when Kubla Khan rode by, vivid pink and yellow posters remind the hill people "We Must Liberate Taiwan."

One more twist of the road, and then you see it, writhing over precipice and crag, wriggling across valleys, and up the hillside into eternity . . . the Great Wall. When you look at this stupendous, stone snake (in places 39 feet high, and 32 feet wide) built by muscle and sweat without the aid of anything much more mechanical than a wheelbarrow, and stretching for 1684 miles, you begin to have some faint glimmering of insight into the unchanging, indomitable character of the Chinese people. Unchanging because I'm completely certain that if Mao Tse-tung were to ask it, his modern Chinese would swarm over these ancient hills and build an exactly similar wall, in exactly the same old way. We stopped at Green Dragon Bridge where the road goes through an archway in the wall, into the vastness beyond, and where the railroad burrows into the mountainside. Muscles aching, hearts pounding we walked along the top of the wall to a watch tower (there's one every 120 feet) where the

signal beacons used to blaze. Here never-sleeping eyes used to look out along the pass between the fierce mountains, and watching archers fiddled impatiently with taut bowstrings.

At last the pitch of the wall was too steep. I began to slither and fall until I took off my treacherous shoes (the same slippery-soled pair that had so nearly broken my ankle for me in San Francisco one day when we tried to walk up to the Mark Hopkins hotel). Ahead and above was another watch tower; and another, and another, and another, and another, climbing away up into the low-sailing clouds, towards the Yellow Sea.

"We go on?" suggested Hu Er Chien, our guide, politely.

There was a pregnant pause while the old walkabouters stared out across the mountains and along the wall, gathering sufficient breath for a reply. Then we had one of those spasms of team telepathy that sometimes cause us to speak spontaneously, in chorus:

"No thanks, Hu," we said, "we've got the picture." And we headed for the Ming Tomb reservoir.

A straggle of tiny teenage girls came marching exultantly, but almost reeling from weariness, up the slope, their tired feet slurring through the powdery dust. They were at the age when western girls would be dreaming of their next date, or of their new party dress. Sweat shone like lacquer on their broad, brown faces, and darkened their work clothes. They carried shovels, and picks over their shoulders; and one of them held aloft a banner on a swaying bamboo rod. Alongside the marchers a fierce, fanatical little peasant girl leader, called the cadence count, shouting new strength into her comrades. Their faces were as radiant as a bride's; these were proud, happy girls, and as they swung past us and disappeared over the rise we heard them start up a song. A song about the glory of working for China.

They had just completed a stint of manual labour on the Ming Tomb reservoir, a tiny section of the 45,000 strong work army that swarms over mountain and valley here every eight hours of every day. When the daylight ebbs the great floodlights take over and the work goes on.

We arrived just at the change of shift, and there were perhaps 100,000 dirty, dedicated people milling around the embankments and camps all along the dry river bed. Golden dust hung like the smoke from a forest fire, over the great plain.

I doubt very much whether history has seen such a spectacle of elementary human endeavour, of man going out barehanded to conquer mountains and rivers, since the building of the pyramids, or perhaps the Great Wall. The reservoir lies in the foothills below Tien Shou Shan (Heavenly Age Hill) where 13 Ming emperors sleep in opulent peace, and its construction has set the imagination of Chinese youth on fire. An overwhelming proportion of all labour on the dam is voluntary. To have done your fortnight here without cracking in the choking dust, or under the inhuman pace set by your leader, is to have climbed Everest, run a four-minute mile, and pitched a World Series shutout. There is always a long waiting list of eager volunteers. And I DO mean volunteers. It is dangerously unreal to imagine these young people as downtrodden, or suppressed. They are completely convinced of their mission, of the very reason for their existence; to work till they drop, and maybe die, for the Forward Leap for China. The present day Chinese is surely the greatest patriot on earth. China is God and Mao is his prophet.

In these long lines of men and youths carrying baskets of stones, shovelling, pounding the earth, and pushing barrows, are taxi-drivers, bankers, hotel bellhops, clerks, soldiers on leave, university students and peasants from faraway farmlands. When Egypt's resident ambassador in Peking wanted to make some picturesque gesture of thanks for Communism's support in the Suez snatch-and-grab he put on a white baseball cap

"On the other hand I suppose it's just as effective for keeping people IN?"

and led his staff out to work as a labourer here on this dam. And the busy cameras of the People's Press scarcely missed a shovelful of the propaganda. The catchment area is three miles long, the retaining wall 29 metres high, and the capacity of the dam 60 million cubic metres. A fair sized job of work in anybody's country, but these determined workers finished it in just six months. No bulldozers, no earth scoops, no tractors, no drills, hardly any mechanical aids at all, just the irresistible force of limitless human energy. Almost the only sign of mechanism (apart from a broken down roller) is a crude, wavering rail-road track along which an ineffectual locomotive sometimes hauls a rake of trucks made from old packing cases. But as often as not the engine founders and a hundred impatient hands start pushing.

There is no concrete anywhere, only rocks (carried from up to a mile away in small baskets) and the brown earth hammered into shape by primitive battering rams. Teams of girls (eight to a team, and not one girl more than 60 inches high) jerk on short ropes in unison, snapping a heavy stone ram head high, then crashing it down on the trembling ground. As they work they gasp out a rhythmic hi-yi-yi chorus. They never stop to spare an aching muscle, they don't pause for smokes or drinks or to wipe perspiration from their smarting eyes. They have never heard of overtime, hardship money, appearance money and all the other articles of western industrial faith. If they did hear them they would despise them as they despise their own weak flesh for yearning for rest after a meagre eight hours' labour. Unwearying and unyielding they work fiercely on, and on, for China.

And this is the gallant picture of China that will stay with us long after the aching drabness, and the lost laughter have been forgotten . . . the picture of those wonderful, exhausted little girls marching home to their hessian huts with glory in their eyes.

For these kids this is no time for frills and femininity. Maybe their grandchildren will be able to think about lipstick and lingerie, but for them there can be no such distraction, there is too much work to be done.

Glamour was Communism's earliest victim in China. You can stroll the cheerless streets of Peking all day, without seeing a skirt or a sign of lipstick; without thrilling to the faintest breath of perfume; without hearing the click of high heels, or catching the glint of legs sheathed in nylon. I don't know whether, at some time they had a drive and exorcised femininity the way they've expunged the sparrows, and mosquitoes, but I suspect that the word was passed around that true beauty

is functional, like a tractor, and that vanity is anti-revolutionary. From that moment forward drabness probably became the badge of patriotism; and, on the great sea of colourless, unpowdered faces, 300 million noses shone proudly for China.

Somewhere along the Rectification trail the skirt, that reactionary garment hinting traitorously at inequality between male and female, was banished with all the other womanly witchcraft, and replaced by denim slacks. You can't get through your work quota so well in high heeled shoes, so out they went, too, to join the other western demons on the sinful side of the joss-stick smoke-screen. The pretty girls of Shanghai hastily evacuated the Bund, and, like the last surviving specimens of some rare and beautiful species, raced across the border to sanctuary in Kowloon.

Just when you are about ready to mourn the old, colourful days of the mandarins, and to conclude that Communism is a withering curse on China's womanhood, you meet a grandmother hobbling awkwardly on ugly little knots of feet, crippled by the ancient practice of foot-binding, while beside her a healthy, glowing granddaughter strides along in the comfort of big, black boots.

In Peking's one modern department store there is a cosmetic counter (presided over by solemn, disapproving little girls with the faces of noviate nuns) where lipstick compacts, nail polish, and all the feminine fripperies are on sale, but though we waited and watched, we never did discover who the customers are. I have the impression that sheer economics, as much as anything, has planted the kiss

of death on the beauty bars. In this land of ruthless realism you think twice before you squander two days' pay on a jar of cold cream.

On Wang Fu Ching (Peking's shopping street) we found a small, dusty window displaying what is possibly the most astonishing collection of millinery in existence. It featured women's hats which might well have blown off the shining curls of the flappers at the Henley Regatta of 1920, and been recovered by boathook from the Thames to reappear here by some secret

"Take it easy—this is the first mountain I've moved in my spare time."

CHAPEAU BY RAILWAY WORKSHOPS ENGINE-DRIVERS UNION

COIFFURE BY THE STATE SHEARERS' CO-OPERATIVE

DRESS JEWELERY IN STREET COMMITTEE BADGES OF OFFICE.

SACK STYLE SWAGGER JACKET IN GAY ALL-WEATHER PADDED CANVAS.

HAUTE MONDE FOR COLLECTIVE FARMERS

MISS PEKING 5

UTILITY MATADOR SLACKS IN LUXURIOUS QUILTED HESSIAN

ACCESSORIES

PARTY LINE PUMPS BY COBBLERS' CO-OPERATIVE

MISS PEKING, 1958:

HOBBIES : WEIGHT-LIFTING, BUILDING BRIDGES

AMBITION: TO ACHIEVE POLITICAL MATURITY THROUGH DILIGENT SOCIAL STUDY

FAVOURITE RECORD: " MY TRACTOR AND I "

FAVOURITE BOOK : " PIG RAISING ON THE COLLECTIVE FARM "

smuggling route through Siberia.

There were excessively jaded looking creations of limp muslin, decorated garishly by rigid, faded roses, and trimmings that may once have been coquettish and gay, but which now looked as sad as the ribbons on an old wreath.

We stood there, two foreigners, hopelessly lost in a strange world where old values and past experiences count for nothing. What prompted some Peking shopkeeper to assemble this incredible array? and what could he possibly hope to gain by it since any true Chinese woman would rather be seen in the stars-and-stripes of the Daughters of the American Revolution than appear in public in this totally outmoded and fiendishly western headgear?

There was worse to come; in a men's store, in elegant solitude, we found a curly-brimmed, shiny top hat of the kind that must have been worn by the diplomats of Legation Row. It was irresistible, a top hat on Wang Fu Ching. We went in, tried it on, according each other coarse western guffaws while the Orient looked on, unsmiling, coldly polite, utterly inscrutable. It didn't fit either of us. Thank heaven.

Some day, fairly soon in China's history, the front office is going to realise the impossibility of sustaining an abnormal society indefinitely, and it's going to have to start a high-pressure campaign to popularise romance among the moppet masses.

Right now, in what is, superficially, a sexless community, boy doesn't meet girl; not in the old hearts-and-flowers sense anyway. The soaring birthrate figures prove of course that biology is having something of a boom period, but it gets no romantic buildup. There are no young couples holding hands in the People's parks; in fact there are no young couples. You see groups of girls, and groups of boys. They don't giggle and glance at each other as jeanagers have done since the beginning of time; and in the movies there's never any danger of two heads merging into one in front of you. The only dates these kids have are with lathes and lecture halls; their only emotional involvement a passion for patriotism. They have also a highly developed phobia about bugs of all sorts; smart teenagers wear surgeons' masks and carry fly swatters; and in this atmosphere of distrust the old love bug is liable to summary liquidation.

Whenever you observe a situation like this, in a land like this, it is all too easy to leap to some conclusion that may be way off the beam. You're very apt to decide that every form of behaviour that varies from our western pattern is something new, some unnatural thing forced on a brainwashed public by soulless dictators reaching for a red moon. The word I have here from impartial people (who don't care two hoots whether or not I believe what they tell me) is that this was never really hand-holding territory and that China was always pretty much Puritan country long before Sun Yat Sen emerged as the new streamlined Confucius.

Just the same I have the sentimental notion that any country (and particularly one that is force-feeding its citizens with culture) needs poetry and music, and literature, and I don't think they're going to get all this without love and romance. Currently the People's poets are churning out

Christmas-cracker verse about tractors and Forward Leaps, but this is unimportant - the literature of expediency.

Skimming through a huge complicated country as rapidly as we are; gulping down impressions like a plowman swallowing a pint, the main problem is to sort out which things happen here because these people live under communism, and which things happen because they were born Chinese.

Was it some curious mental block in the new China's approach to the boy-girl relationship that made such a big production of the now famous international incident concerning the London business man the waitress and the Penguin book? Or would it have worked out just the same way when the mandarins rode the sedan chair trails?

What happened was that John F. (a friend of ours from

London staying in Peking for technical discussions with the government) had lunch one day in the Swedish bar of the Hsinchiao hotel. He was waited on with her usual amiable efficiency by a pint-sized little waitress whom we all liked and whom we all called "Button." The language barrier restricted our friendship with her to wide grins. Button is about four feet nine in her stockings (which are a grisly shade of pink artificial silk and which she rolls around a garter below her knee so that she looks vaguely like some bizarre character in a Shakespearean play) and she has about her the same urgent aura of sex-appeal as a stone statue of the late Queen Victoria.

As John rose to leave the dining room Button raced to the door, held it open for him, and gave him the customary wide smile. Feeling that some reciprocal gesture was called for, John grinned back cheerfully and tapped her lightly on the head with the Penguin book he was carrying. Had he attempted to carry her off, struggling, into the canebreak, he could hardly have touched off more indignation.

He was summoned to the Ministry of Foreign Affairs, sternly lectured on the deadly sin of raising a hand to a woman and ordered to apologise.

Observed his pal, Joe (who had gone along as a witness, or something), closing the incident tactfully: "Good Heavens, what a lot of fuss about nothing; why at home when we are pleased with a waitress we strike her to the ground." The Ministry was not amused.

The big thing that all tourists have in common (apart from cameras, colour-film, and loud voices) is the firm conviction that they aren't tourists. And there are no more stubborn victims of this odd fixation than those chronic ever-orbiting, old walkabouters Rigby and Ward. We pass by parks and palaces, tombs and

scenic wonders with sophisticated shudders. "Tourist stuff," we say, disdainfully, frantically fumbling for our light meters.

A guide has merely to announce "We now come to the inner temple of the goddess of heavenly purity, built in the year . . ." to send us racing for cover, hands clamped over our ears. So it was with some mild surprise that we found ourselves leaning over a rail in the Peking Zoo, gazing into the unblinking eyes of a giant panda. Tourist stuff, sure enough, but this was tourism with a twist, because all the other panda-starers were Mongolians, Cantonese and Manchurians. In all the wide zoological gardens we were the only two specimens of homo europeanus on view; and even the characters in the cages weren't more cut off by lack of language than we were.

The first little contretempts occurred at the ticket box where Riggers held up a sullen, muttering queue while he made like a bush ballader reciting The Wild Colonial Boy. The little pigtailed girl didn't understand Australian, so she replied curtly in Chinese, and handed him two coin-like tokens which, with consummate skill he instantly mixed with all the loose change in his pocket, then strolled towards the turnstile humming a few bars from his favourite aria. Or vice versa.

At the turnstile another solemn little girl, with the inevitable twin plaits of braided black hair, rejected our clumsy attempts to pass by, sternly sent us back to the end of the box-office queue. It turned out that the coins which we'd thought were part of the change, were in fact, admission tokens to be presented at the gate. By now the girls had decided to take charge of these helpless foreign males who couldn't even speak Mandarin and who might turn out to be Russian. They took all our change, sorted through it briskly, found the two admission tokens, gave us back our money, then shepherded us contemptuously into the gardens. We looked back and found them giving us the long, slow stare that hinted at the imminence of a rush call to Secret Police HQ.

The Communists claim in a handbook that, before Rectification, the rotters of the old regime (though with typical cynicism they called this zoo The Garden of Ten Thousand Lives) had allowed the establishment to dwindle to "a dozen starved monkeys, two parrots, and a one-eyed ostrich." Now there are more than 1,000 birds and animals, all living in hygienic concrete cells, and at the last eyesight test the ostrich scored 6/6 on the chart.

Comrades, have you checked your zoo lately? Anybody been to the Bronx to check the ostrich's eyes?

The only inmate of Peking Zoo still seemingly in need of a little re-education is an Australian black swan swimming around the lake in a reactionary sort of way.

Right next door to the zoo is perhaps the most significant building, or group of buildings in Peking . . . the Soviet Exhibition Centre. Its minarets and turrets (ornate and ostentatious) are clustered round a tall, gilded spire topped by a gleaming red star which can be seen for miles. There is a theatre seating 3,000, a cinema seating 800, and a restaurant that can handle 400 people at a sitting. And it is as permanent in appearance as the Kremlin itself.

There now arose a tricky problem. We had been delivered to the gates of the zoo by a taxi, which had then high-tailed it back to Peking, some five miles away. But now, as far as the eye could see, there were no taxis. True, there were plenty of buses, but to strangers who have only a vague notion of the direction in which they want to travel; who don't know where to get off; and who can't ask anyone directions, these were but a minor comfort. Most men would face a firing squad rather than make fools of themselves publicly and we are among this haughty group, but at last we

gritted our teeth and sprang
into a bus where about 60
citizens watched with interest
while we offered coins, notes,
shrugs, grins and gestures. The
bus rolled on endlessly, we
changed conductors, we paid
more fares, and were resigned
to circling round Peking's
outer suburbs until our visas
expired when the conductress
stopped the bus and turned
us over to some pedicab men
who spoke enough English to
get us home.

Who needs a guide? Not us,
it's tourist stuff.

"It's so nice the way everyone's so FRIENDLY at breakfast time."

PUNCTUALLY at 8.30 each morning every head in the Hsinchiao dining-room swivels. A slim, smart woman in tailored slacks comes in and sits at a table by the broad window where she can look out over the grey, dusty city that she loves. She has the hard-to-pinpoint grace of the Chinese women of the old regime. Not the padded shapelessness of modern Peking, but the elegance of the Chinese girls in the cheong sums at, say, a Hong Kong jockey club meeting.

"Han Suyin," whispers the Hsinchiao grapevine. "She wrote A Many Splendoured Thing; but don't try to talk to her, she keeps herself aloof, she'll brush you off."

She didn't look aloof to us; just pleasantly poised, so we

talked to her, and found that she laughs easily, as we do, at the same things that we do; and we became good friends.

Han Suyin (a graduate of London University) was born here in Peking, but she's half European, half Chinese, and now practises medicine in Singapore. Her husband, an official of the old, hated Kuomintang regime, was killed in the civil war against the Communists.

"When he died," she said, "all my friends expected me to kill myself, to starve myself to death, like a good widow should; but I didn't, and they were shocked. That's what China was like in those times."

It seemed to us that here, over the breakfast coffee, and through the mellow haze of the first cigarette of the day, we might find the magic-formula for movie success; for here was the girl with the golden touch on a typewriter. Hollywood bids high for her stories before she's finished writing them, before they've even seen a rough plot outline. She must surely know her way round the Beverly Hill jungles and the movie studios like a native, she must know every trick in the fabulous trade. "No" she said, "I've never been to Hollywood, though I hope to go, and I didn't have anything to do with the filming. I just sent them the story and forgot about it. I've seen the movie and I like it. You see, I'm not really a proper writer at all, I'm a doctor. I just write in my spare time."

"So you learned by studying movie technique, by watching thousands of movies, by analysing and dissecting until you hit on the formula?"

Dr. Han laughed the laugh that had made us like her so quickly, "No; I see about two movies a year, and then they're usually very old ones. I don't like movies much."

What's she doing in Peking, this world traveller, a sophisticate, a woman of the Kuomintang days?

Her father, who died recently, left her six houses here, thus making her a capitalist in Red China, and every day she goes dauntlessly off to argue with officials, about titles, rents, rates and taxes. The big problem they're struggling with? Well Han Suyin doesn't much want to be a Peking capitalist; she doesn't need the rent income; and she doesn't want to be bothered with the responsibilities of a landlord, so her idea is to give these houses to the government. Can't be done, they insist, it isn't proper, the book doesn't say anything about giving houses away. Every morning Dr. Han goes off to explain to officialdom that she can't do much about a leaky roof in Peking when she's in a Singapore surgery, or maybe in a Hollywood studio; and that she's just got to get those houses off her hands, and off her mind. They shake their heads stubbornly, these are her houses, aren't they? Her father left them to her, didn't he? Well, the book says . . .

Communism may be (thought this I doubt) a sometime thing here, but China and the Chinese are for ever.

PROBABLY no feature of the Chinese pattern, from Confucius to comrades, is more permanent than the Peking Opera. We went there with a linguist from the British Embassy (who offered to translate for us), the engineer who's trying to sell free-piston engines, a Reuters' man, and Lady Burton. (She is a devoted archaeologist who has been entertaining faint hopes that the government might allow her to join in the current excavation of one of the famous Ming tombs. But the government is keeping this project as secret as the H-bomb formula.)

As a young man I was an opera lover; I was also a movie lover, a park bench lover, and a front-gate lover. I was a lover wherever it was dark enough. Later when increasing age made romance nothing more than a semi-senile giggle in my memory, I became a fairly sound opera sleeper. What I am trying to establish here is that you are dealing with an operatic authority because I feel it my duty to report that, in my book, the Peking Opera, which has survived centuries of social upheavals, is strictly for the birds.

The Opera House (naturally it is called The People's Opera House for everything here carries that reassuring tag) is an imposing building with the tall columns and flights of broad stone stairs that opera seems to call for, but the moment you step inside the tone drops sharply. You are confronted with a railway-station type display of all the familiar candy and gum. At least you think you are until you move a little closer and discover that every label is a copy of some widely advertised western one with only the name altered. The notion that the Japanese are

the world's foremost copyists may have to be revised when Chinese production hits its peak.

Where I come from you put on white tie and tails to go to the opera, and you go whether you're tone-deaf or not, because attending operas is a sure sign that you are no peasant. It is a sort of compulsory social parade to show all your friends that you're just as cultured as they are, deep down in your heart.

In Peking they play it differently. They go either

because they want to or because there just isn't any other way of filling in the evening without breaking a back bending over a lathe. And what they wear to a first night is the same as they wear for everything else from meeting Mao to hunting house-sparrows, navy blue boiler suits. And they give opera pretty much the same treatment as they give everything else; the long, slow stare served up absolutely deadpan.

The only time they laughed, or applauded was when a mildly comical character turned a few somersaults and twirled a sort of drum major's baton. It turned out that he was the only one in the cast who spoke a dialect that the masses could understand; the others were giving out with the nasal, high-pitched traditional opera stuff and these sturdy comrades just didn't have a clue as to what they were talking about.

Modern Chinese dramatists sometimes hit on a new theme (there was one satirical play running while we were there, all about America's early sputnik failures, with Eisenhower in a wheelchair), but the old-timers of the opera never do. Their operatic plots are even older and more fatuous than the evergreens of Covent Garden and Milan.

The big one, the one that's been their meal ticket right back to the Mings is a dramatic deal known as Monkey plays. There are some hundreds of variations on one of the thinnest plot frames in playwriting history, but basically they are all about a monkey which, for some reason or other, starts on a Marco Polo type journey and meets up with complications. The monkey business we saw showed the poor old monk having trouble with a flame-spurting mountain range that was bottle-necking his entire trip. Some picturesque rascal tips him off (in a scene lasting about 45 minutes) that the only way to sneak through these red-hot rocks is to get possession of the magic fan. And guess who has the magic fan? Only the beautiful princess, that's who.

My Mandarin is a little limited for an operatic critic. I can say "Please bring me a cold beer; Third floor; small cat, and don't mention it," but even this comprehensive collection didn't help me to grasp the finer points. As far as I can see nobody ever stays right through one of these operas because when a monkey play really gets going it is liable to run all summer and the action is so arranged that it doesn't matter much when you decide to walk in, or out.

The story is so frail that anyone above moron level gets the general message in two minutes flat at any point in the production.

Costumes and mime are superb, the singing excruciating, and the acting first class. Every gesture, every detail of dress and makeup has its own special significance. It wouldn't surprise me to learn that our original western horse opera was based on the Peking model of stark simplicity and a highly unflattering estimate of the mental capacity of the audience because where the western villain always wears a black hat so the Peking badee always has a black beard. Anywhere along the peanut and popcorn trail black means trouble.

The people here sit in the big, bare theatre in polite silence. They must be the world's best-behaved audiences. They don't cough

"WHADDEESAY? WHADDEESAY?"

and shuffle and scrape their feet as our theatre-goers do; they don't whisper to each other, or rustle programmes, or crumple candy wrappers. And (remembering my good old operatic days) I took a few swift peeks into the darkness of the back stalls. You know what? These characters aren't opera lovers at all . . . they don't even hold hands.

IT WAS our last night in Peking and the party at the British legation had gone on for so long that now it wasn't worthwhile going to bed. Our plane for Canton was due to leave in an hour with the coming of daylight, so we were walking back, through the empty streets, to the hotel.

Our footfalls echoed eerily along the high, prison-like walls of the embassies up and down "Legation Row"; and, for a long time, there was no other sound. It was almost impossible to realise that this was a city of three million people, a city bigger than any we knew on our own wide mainland, for it was as silent as the Australian bush.

In Hong Kong, or Kowloon, or Singapore men would have come quickly out from the furtive side-streets, trotting alongside persistently, offering insidious invitations of swift transport to secret bars and dens. Soft-footed beggars would have fallen in behind us, keeping only the length of their own ragged shadows away, following as relentlessly as vultures, and jasmine-scented romance would have been pathetically and persistently on sale at every corner. In Peking, it seemed, we were utterly alone.

No cars tooted now; no headlights sliced the darkness; no merrymakers staggered boisterously home with the milk. But after a little while we became aware that the city wasn't as sleepy as it seemed. At almost every block there was a grey sentry box, and as we strolled by with bogus nonchalance, we could feel cold eyes watching us. A platoon of soldiers came marching down the street towards us, a little patch of khaki in the growing greyness, their soft-soled boots

slithering over the ground. They had rifles slung over their shoulders. They looked uncomfortably like a firing squad. And our consciences were heavy with guilt, because we had, for the past week or so, been haunting a tiny little bar in the maze and muddle of the Peking markets which, we had recently learned, was once notorious as a hangout and meeting place for spies and international riffraff. The Peaceful Winds they call it, and we liked it because it offered some slight escape from the prevailing gloom. You could get a cold beer there, and listen to very old, very scratchy records of Benny Goodman, or the Hot Club of France. (Once I stopped at a record shop in the markets thinking I might buy a typical Chinese song, for some of them are as beautiful as bird-song, but all I could find were stacks of records of the Soviet national anthem.) The soldiers trudged by, eyeing us steadily, and we sweated, but they went shuffling off on some mysterious mission.

You hear all sorts of rumours here, of the three shots that ring out at dawn each day behind high walls. You hear of re-education at revolver point; and a foreign journalist, just finishing long residence in Peking, swore that he'd seen, only recently, a truck load of prisoners, hands tied behind their backs, jolting over the rough streets to a dawn appointment with death.

These are the rumours that ricochet softly round the walls of this rumour-rife city, and it would be presumptuous for us, after so brief a visit, to attempt to confirm or deny them; but on this silent dawn, as we went through the sleeping streets, we heard no shots, and met no condemned men.

No-one stopped us to query what two foreigners were doing strolling around at such a suspicious hour in a capital where there is no night life to make sense of such behaviour. No-one gave us a good night or a good morning; nobody made any sign that they recognised our existence. The sentries and the policemen just stared, taking in every detail of our appearance, and as their eyes raked our backs I suddenly remembered wildly the book that was even now, on the table in our hotel room.

Some humourist had lent it to me, and its title was The Spies Bedside Book. It's a Grahame Green anthology of espionage, containing all the details of spy technique, as well as comical advertisements for false moustaches, invisible ink, and elaborate disguises. At the time it had seemed to be richly humorous, but now it suddenly lost a lot of its laughter.

I wondered what I would do if the room-boy had turned this piece of damning evidence in to the security police, and if they (as was highly probable) had no sense of humour. Perhaps I would refer them to Chou-en-lai's former personal assistant Chang whom we had interviewed that afternoon.

He is a slim, scholarly man who speaks English with the ease of one who must surely have spent long years overseas. Though he wore the inevitable navy blue tunic he was worldly and friendly, one of the very few Chinese in Peking who didn't seem to belong to some other, impenetrable world.

"Well," he said. "Has it been worthwhile? Have you seen everything you want to see? Met everyone you want to meet?" And then he grinned the delightful grin which these mysterious people offer with such tragic infrequence to westerners: "Do you feel as if you've been behind a bamboo curtain?"

We struggled between caution, politeness, and honesty: "No," we told him, "we don't. But we feel as if we're walking on tiptoe all the time."

There were no guards waiting at the Hsinchiao to drag

"Oh, don't bother gentlemen, we can find our own way out."

us away to the dungeons. The room boys had assembled our baggage in the lobby and were getting anxious that we might miss the plane. Seeing them gathered there in the old hotel farewell formation it was hard to resist the habit of handing out tips, but we knew that to do so would be to offer a deadly insult.

Railway stations and quays used to be the loneliest spots on earth; bleak little outposts of human misery perpetually tinged with melancholy, but now, I think, no place is so hopelessly impregnated with the sadness of a million goodbyes as an airport. Peking though, was merciful (as afterwards Kowloon and Tokyo were not). There were no friends to be snatched away from us, brutally, and for ever at the barrier; no familiar features among the curious faces pressed against the wire mesh fence. We left easily, without a pang.

The usual shrill little voice came riding out, like a witch on a broomstick, from the public address system, across halls and waiting rooms, shouting a message in Chinese. "Come on," said Han Suyin, who was flying south, too, and who had become our fairy godmother for this trip. "That's us, off we go."

We crowded into a Russian aircraft that looked like a cross between a Convair and a Dakota, finding seats on the first-come-first-served principle as though it were a streetcar. Inside it was austere and strictly functional. There were safety belts, but no-one told us to use them, and no signs flashed to give the usual takeoff warnings. Peking slid away from us beneath a layer of steamy cloud, and we settled down to face the boredom of an eight-hour flight.

We were more than half an hour behind schedule as we landed at Cheung Chow and taxied in past long lines of dispersal bays, each one sheltering a tiny MIG jet fighter. We figured that we must have struck headwinds, but presently, as we glumly sipped scalding yellow tea, came an announcement: "Engine trouble," translated Suyin. "They now have to fly a new motor either from Peking or Canton. They say we may be stuck here overnight."

This was pre-noon; we looked at Cheung Chow and quailed, but we were held there for only five hours, and as we waited Han Suyin told us about China. We had always wondered how such tremendous efficiency and mass discipline was achieved among people who can't read.

"Further proof of the freedom of the people—even seat belts aren't compulsory."

"Street committees," she explained. "Supposing, for example, you're a rather lazy person and that you don't keep your backyard clean and free from flies and rats and mosquitoes, well, you'll be certain to get a visit from your street leader. She (it's generally a she) will be pleasant and friendly. She'll talk about your children, and she'll perhaps drink tea with you and gradually she'll work the conversation round to communal efforts and tidiness and hygiene and then she'll mention that your yard needs cleaning up. If you don't do anything about it she'll call again and this time may offer to help you with the job. Then if you're still unco-operative you'll find that your neighbours suddenly stop talking to you and that you're ostracised."

We all argued mildly, and amiably about the ethics of this polite squeeze play, so typical of the sweet-and-sour methods that make China's Communism work. Most of us were shocked at the terrible loss of privacy, the privilege which democracy's citizens value so highly.

Here in this old-new land a desire for privacy is suspect. If you're so keen to be alone, to hide your deeds and thoughts from your neighbours then, without a doubt, you're a counter-revolutionary, or any way in need of drastic re-education. So the street leader takes to dropping in on you unexpectedly, rather like a gang boss in the old protection-racket days calling on a prospective client, suggesting in one way and another that you fall in line . . . or else.

Someone calls to talk to you about Family Planning (birth control), and someone else drops by to have a friendly talk with you about ways of

improving your work quota
at the factory; yet another
someone pops in to mention,
in a comradely way, that your
roof is the only one in the street
without a scarecrow, and that
the anti-sparrow drive is only
two days off.

Even if you are only a
half-smart cookie you get the
message. Conform comrade. So
you plan your family, you step
up your output at the factory;
and you build the biggest
scarecrow on the block. And
for all I know, in doing all this,
in playing ball with every do-
gooder who knocks on your
door, you may find happiness,
I wouldn't know. I tried hard,
but I never did find out much
about happiness in China.
There is palpable pride there,
and patriotism, and wonderful
self-sacrifice, but happiness is
something else again. It is a deep-
down thing, and I couldn't find
out about it, one way or the other.

"Anxious to leave? WHO'S anxious to leave?"

LO WU:

On page 16 of our passports there is a blue-inked impression of a rubber stamp about the size of an Australian shilling piece. Compared with all the other seals and coats-of-arms, it doesn't look particularly impressive, but it is, without doubt, the most important of all the dozens of stamps in the book, for this is our exit visa, the magic sign that allows us to pass back over the bridge at Shumchun into the friendly familiar chaos of democracy.

Standing once more in the blow-torch sunlight on the platform at Shumchun, with our baggage piled on the gravel beside us, we can look straight along the railroad track and see the promised land beyond the frontier guards, the New Territories of Hong Kong.

We know that our papers are in order; we know that there is nothing sinister in our bags for the customs men to discover; we're not trying to smuggle Chinese currency out, or works of art, or corpses, or unexposed film. We know that it is absurd to be so tense, so impatient. But why the hell are they taking so long to go through our papers? We see in exasperation our connecting train moving off towards Kowloon without us. We wait and wait. Everyone is pleasant, and polite, but nothing that we can do or say seems to speed things up.

Then, suddenly, we're walking over the bridge towards the unostentatious little Union Jack. The Chinese guards don't even glance at us, and we don't look back. A smart Hong Kong policeman (conspicuously without a sub-machine gun) sees the word "British" on our passports and waves us on hospitably, "This way, sir," he says, and we cross the border.

You have to travel a mile into the New Territories before you notice much change in scene or atmosphere because that last mile by the frontier is a no-man's land of minefields, but at the first whistle stop along the line a Chinese girl ripples down the aisle of the train on high heels, with an elegance and grace that makes Monroe's wiggle look like a ploughboy's slouch. She leaves a faint trail of perfume behind her; and she wears the most glamorous feminine garment ever devised . . . the cheong sum. Just one mile back her sisters are navy-blue nonentities, distinguishable from their menfolk only by their plaits.

(The cheong sum is a one-piece, form-fitting sheath of a dress with a high collar that sets off to perfection the long slender beauty of a Chinese neck; and with a drastically slit skirt that sets off to perfection the long slender beauty of a Chinese leg. Somebody once remarked that the cheong sum was the east's answer to the plunging neckline; but it isn't just an answer, it's a crushing rejoinder.)

When you come back from a trip like this you begin, instinctively, looking for dramatic differences, and it's probable that most of the ones you notice are imaginary, but now even the schoolchildren seem rowdier, less inhibited. We remember the kids we saw in Canton going to school, walking sedately two by two, hand in hand, all singing some cheery Forward Leap song with a young leader to remind them of the words. Here in the New Territories the schoolchildren don't march, they scuffle and scramble and push each other. They behave badly as individuals always behave.

There are rows of cars parked beneath the trees at very halt now; there is colour, dazzling, delightful colour in the dress of the people; and the road that runs alongside the track is black, with the familiar white line down the middle.

Now we're in Kowloon and the flash bulbs are popping for authoress Han Suyin (who has been promising herself all the way down that she would sneak past the press gang by pretending to be our interpreter). We abandon her callously and rush out to drink in the wonderful bustle of Kowloon; the endless chain of double-decker buses (bright red like the London ones) and the hurrying crowds making for the Star ferry. All along Nathan road the cabs, green, yellow and red, weave recklessly among the thick traffic; the shops are bulging with opulent merchandise. The place is vibrant with life.

At night when the lights dance up the peaks of Hong Kong island and reflect in the water of the harbour; when they glitter like diamonds all over Kowloon and dim the starlight, we look back, at last to the hazy blue hills of the land we have left forever, waiting for the sight of it to stir some mood, some emotion. But China remains stubbornly as remote from us and as inexplicable as the moon.

"Us? Brainwashed? Heavens, NO!"

PERTH: *A Sydney citizen, returning from London looked through the window of the Super Constellation as we taxied into Perth Airport and uttered a gag so old that it was probably originally cracked in sanskrit: "Western Australia, the land of sin, sand, and sorrow," he said; and in the telepathic chorus which is becoming habitual with, Riggers and I fervently replied, "She'll do me."*

Less than nine hours before we had been sweating in Singapore's steam-bath climate, out shirts blotchy with damp, rank with impending mildew. Perth's air was clean and cool though the sun shone in a cloudless blue sky and the slight chill of the early morning was like a welcoming hug to wanderers who had tasted too much summer, in too many lands. We had been north, as far as China's great wall, by way of Singapore, Bangkok, Hong Kong and Peking. Then south again to the glitter of Hong Kong, and the comfortable confusion of Kowloon. Out from Hong Kong harbour, sneaking between the islands, and the junk fleets, to gamble in Macao, and to see there once more the ominous sentries on Red China's border. Across the China Sea to Japan (in fewer than five hours by Britannia's Whispering Giant) to wander along the glamorous Ginza under the blaze of Tokyo's dazzling midnight, to meander up through the mountains, to sit on the shores of Lake Kawaguchi and watch the lightning crackle around the snowy summit of Fujiyama.

Now, at last, we were home, and the toughest assignment of our careers was behind us. Tough because, generally speaking, we are pretty flippant characters, playing life strictly for laughs, and Red China happens to be fresh out of laughter right now. And because, in all the countries we visited (those eager, over-populated countries of the Asia from which we illogically exclude ourselves), there is very little for any intelligent Australian to laugh about.

Tough, too, because telling the truth, as you see it, is one of those dead-loss propositions where you just can't win.

The big question, of course, the one that everyone outside Red China asks, as if we were holding out on them, is:

"What was it really like in there?"

In a few bustling weeks of observation no-one could say, authoritatively, what the new China is like. The country is vast and its people are complex. All we can offer are impressions like these: - Somehow (whether by murder, magic, or mesmerism we don't know), 600 million people of hopelessly differing dialects, background, and beliefs have suddenly been unified into one of the most single-minded, dedicated nations on earth. A

nation obviously mass-disciplined; obviously healthy, not obviously unhappy; indoctrinated from the kindergarten; deliberately kept out of communication with the west; maliciously misinformed; a nation seemingly satisfied with the way things are; clearly bitterly conscious of the scandalous way things were. A nation primitive and backward beyond the imagination of a western citizen with his time-payment TV, his hire-purchase car, his garden, his mortgage and his washing machine; a nation that has reduced crime to a point never previously approached by any class, creed, or cult. An eager, ambitious nation, thirsty for knowledge, impatient for progress, poised precariously between international friendship and cosmic spite; a nation far too occupied with its urgent tasks to bother about either yet. A nation fanatically dedicated to justice for the masses, yet ruthlessly denying it to the individual. A nation cutting down the gap of centuries with a speed that is at once thrilling and terrifying. From these conflicting impressions one thought emerges and persists . . . to refuse to recognise this nation is as unreal as refusing to acknowledge the existence of the Pacific Ocean.

www.ingramcontent.com/pod-product-compliance
Lightning Source LLC
Chambersburg PA
CBHW081700120626
46550CB00010B/2959